"This is the story of a woman who found the courage through faith, love, and prayer to do extraordinary things. It's written in such a charming, unassuming way that its message sneaks up on us – that we can awaken our own courage and, together, change the world."

Betty Sue Flowers, *editor* of Joseph Campbell's *The Power of Myth* and *Director,* LBJ Library, Austin, TX

"Awakening Courage is a personal journey along the path from simple cross-cultural awareness to compassion, and finally to political action. Shartle's accounts of solidarity with "distant neighbors," entwined with and strengthened by stories of familial relationships, will serve as both comfort and challenge to her readers. This is a personal memoir that will touch and inspire others to transform their compassion into effective action.

Jim Wallis
Editor of *Sojourners* and *Convener* of *Call to Renewal*

"Gretchen Lara Shartle has written a luminous account of how ordinary human sensitivity can lead us to courageous acts of justice. What is truly impressive is that she has turned her life of family privilege into a life of compassion for neighbors near and far. In the process she has learned that compassion is not effective unless it is constantly exposed to the nasty realities of social conflict, whether we are dealing with conditions as near as the local neighborhood or as distant as India, Mexico or Central America. The book is a testimonial narritive of what she has learned and done. Who knows, reading it may lead you to a fresh experience of awakening courage."

Walter Wink, Professor of Biblical Interpretation
Auburn Theological Seminary, New York

Awakening Courage
One Woman's Journey

Gretchen Lara Shartle

Illuminations Press
Calistoga, California

WWW.AWAKENINGCOURAGE.COM

also by Gretchen Lara Shartle

On Earth and In Heaven

Illuminations Press Box 667 Calistoga CA 94515

Library of Congress Control Number: 2003100253
ISBN 0-937088-27-7

5

For Kyria and Greta

in admiration
for their own awakening courage

To a dear friend
whom I hope
to meet.

Dudchen Lara Shtutt

The coming to life of Awakening Courage

Without Betty Sue Flowers' encouragement, I would not have had the confidence to write this book. I am also indebted to Lois Silverstein of Berkeley for coming as close as any person to mid-wifing this project. She did not spare me the labor pains. Instead, she helped me channel them to bring about the birth. Anne Corcos, Ivan and Sarah Diamond allowed me to stay in their homes during the early days. Prominent assistants in this process of mid-wifing have been Nina Diamond, Betty Ellerbee, JoLynn Free, John Henneberger, Judith Liro, Standish Meacham, Karen Paup, Louisa Serafim, Nancy Scanlan, Rosa Shand, Frank Sugeno, Mary Teague and June Keener-Wink.

I worked with Elizabeth Becker to put on the finishing touches, Don Crowell helped me to settle on the name, *Awakening Courage*. And, my beloved Jorge – even while in pain from a persistent illness and, at the time, hardly able to stand, accompanied me step by step. Gene Dekovic and Rana Pierucci were invaluable collaborators in bringing *Awakening Courage* unto the light.

My Family Tree

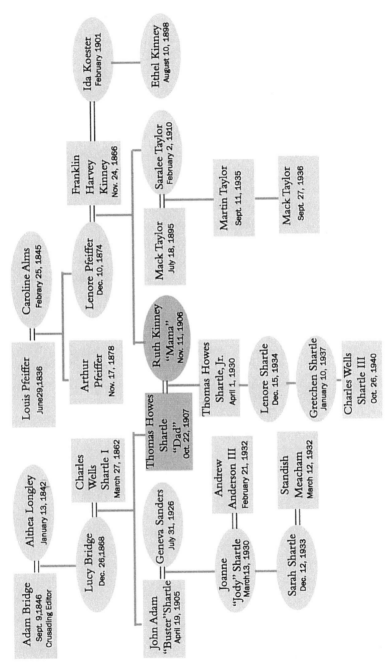

Ida Koester
February 1901

Ethel Kinney
August 10, 1898

Franklin Harvey Kinney
Nov. 24, 1866

Caroline Alms
Febrary 25, 1845

Louis Pfeiffer
June 29, 1836

Lenore Pfeiffer
Dec. 10, 1874

Arthur Pfeiffer
Nov. 17, 1878

Saralee Taylor
February 2, 1910

Mack Taylor
July 18, 1895

Martin Taylor
Sept. 11, 1935

Mack Taylor
Sept. 27, 1936

Ruth Kinney
"Mama"
Nov. 11, 1906

Thomas Howes Shartle
"Dad"
Oct. 22, 1907

Thomas Howes Shartle, Jr.
April 1, 1930

Lenore Shartle
Dec. 15, 1934

Gretchen Shartle
January 10, 1937

Charles Wells Shartle III
Oct. 26, 1940

Althea Longley
January 13, 1842

Adam Bridge
Sept. 9, 1846
Crusading Editor

Charles Wells Shartle I
March 27, 1862

Lucy Bridge
Dec. 26, 1868

Geneva Sanders
July 31, 1926

John Adam
"Buster" Shartle
April 19, 1905

Andrew Anderson III
February 21, 1932

Joanne "Jody" Shartle
March 13, 1930

Standish Meacham
March 12, 1932

Sarah Shartle
Dec. 12, 1933

Contents

Prologue

My Path to Joy

Share your bread with the hungry,

    and bring the homeless poor into your house;

    when you see the naked, cover them —

Then, your light shall break forth like the dawn,

    and your healing shall spring up quickly . . .

(Isaiah 58:7-9)

This is the story of my discovery that each of us can do marvelous things when we join with others to reach out to neighbors near and far. All of our lives will be changed. Discovering this has been like coming upon a secret, a secret that has brought me so much joy that I want to shout it from the rooftops.

1

Planted in a Good Place

I grew up outside Houston, Texas, in the 1940's, eight miles
from town, amid tall pines that were icons of strength for me.
In that place, I became so firmly anchored that I got the confidence to meet strangers without fear. In that place, I found
the determination to realize visions, even those that appeared
to be beyond me. It was there that I began to dream of reaching beyond myself to distant neighbors.

Surrounded by my parents' love in that home in the middle
of those woods, I might have remained happily asleep to the
world for years, but for a jolt I got when I was a year old. Aunt
Ethel's husband, who had been gassed in World War I, died of
tuberculosis in 1938, the year after I was born. Mother left my
older brother, my sister and me for six months to go on a trip
with her sister, who was in mourning. Brother Tommy, was
eight, sister Lenore, was three, and my younger brother, Charles,
had not yet been born.

Though it may not seem like such a big thing to have been
left by Mama when there were other people to take care of me,
I realized many years later what a powerful impact that experience had on me. It left me with a deep apprehension about loss

and separation. I still remember how scared I was to take a nap alone when I was four, five, and six years old. I dreaded the moment after lunch when Mama would say, "It's time to go upstairs for your nap." I was so frightened that I devised a way to help me cope. It had to be something I could visualize – something completely engaging that would leave no room for my fears. I used to rock back and forth on my knees as I looked at my bedroom door and repeated a mantra – "shut the door and open the door, shut the door and open the door." I invented this phrase and said it over and over to stop my mind from worrying. These thoughts, I now believe, were sparked by the fears generated by Mama's long trip.

Those days, Mother and Dad were in their thirties. I had learned to add ten to thirty. That made forty, and forty seemed very old to me. We didn't have the large family base both my parents had had in Ohio, where they grew up, nor did we have a "generational cushion," since all my grandparents had died before I was born. I decided not to talk with Mother about my worries, because I didn't want to frighten her. Also, my big brother had taught me it was babyish to tell anyone when I was afraid. It seemed to me that my only alternative was to try to talk to God.

The first time I was inspired to do this was when I noticed how Mama's hands used to break out in red splotches that hurt and itched. Around age four I wrote a note in pencil asking God to be sure to heal Mama's hands. (Years later, she learned that allergies to certain foods had caused her hands to break out that way.)

Mama used to read a children's prayer book to me that began with the words, "Thank you for the world so sweet." Then she listened as I prayed for everyone in our family and all our animals and anyone who was having a hard time.

Sometimes when she told me stories about her relatives, I would untangle her curls and pull out her gray hairs, carefully, one by one, hoping it might make her live longer. I remember her telling me about her Uncle Arthur who was the only doctor on a ship with five hundred wounded and shell-shocked men when he came home from the first World War. His experiences at the front in Europe and on that ship moved him to open his heart and ultimately to give his life to others. In spite of his family's disapproval, he decided to stop being a doctor for affluent patients and instead to live in the Italian ghetto of Cincinnati in order to serve the poor, people that I now call distant neighbors. Soon after that, the flu epidemic hit. Uncle Arthur caught the virus and died in 1920, at the age of forty-two. Mother later wrote about this in her autobiography, saying, "His death was the first tragedy that shook me to the roots."

I connected the stories about Uncle Arthur to the experiences of soldiers in World War II. From the time I was around six until I was eight years old, I used to imagine our soldiers in concentration camps being tortured, or gassed as Uncle Bob was, or being shot in battles. Mother often went over to the Red Cross in Houston to cut bandages. Gas rationing, food rationing, blackouts at night, Mother's stories and her volunteer work, all made me think about the soldiers at the front in Europe.

Among Dad's ancestors, one of my favorites is his maternal grandfather, Adam Bridge. He was a devout Lutheran who grew up in poverty, then struggled to raise his nine children. Though he had begun his life as a poor man, in 1905, when he turned fifty-nine years old he was able to buy *The Franklin News,* a local newspaper, and to make it one of the most respected papers in the Miami Valley of Ohio. Because of his spirited defense of the poor, people called him "the crusading editor." By publicizing the facts, Adam Bridge kept citizens informed, thus empowering them to stand up for themselves and for others by voting, writing letters, and speaking out to their representatives. Dad's sister, my Aunt Louise, told me how Adam Bridge prayed, "Come, Lord Jesus, and be our guest," before every meal during the years he spent living with my Shartle grandparents.

Mother and Dad seldom read the Bible and hardly ever prayed, except when Mother said prayers with me before I went to sleep at night. Probably it was because of my early experiences with loneliness and my fear of my parents' dying, that I felt drawn to learn more about Jesus' life and death, especially his resurrection. I even staged an experiment to find out what really happened after Jesus died. When I was around nine years old, I found a dead downy yellow chick inside the incubator, which was located in the milk shed beside the barn. I decided to take it to the animal graveyard and to bury it there. After three days, I dug into the hole to see if the chick was gone. Being so practical, I expected it to be there, but I hoped it would be gone.

It was still in its grave. If only it had disappeared, I could more easily have hoped that even if my parents did die, they would always exist somewhere. It would also have made it easier for me to believe in the resurrection. Believing Jesus had actually risen would have assured me that God was close. The fact that the chick was there was disappointing, but it didn't stop me from continuing to search for the truth about God.

I used to wonder what God wanted me to do with my life. When I asked Mama's sister, Aunt Ethel, she encouraged me to pray. Aunt Ethel had become a Christian Scientist after her husband died. Noticing a certain shininess in her face made me want to learn where it came from. When I visited her, I saw that she disappeared every morning for an hour. She went into her room and shut the door. When I asked what she did in there, she said, "I go to a special place in my bedroom, where I do the Christian Science readings and pray."

Inspired by Aunt Ethel, I picked out a large oak tree in our

yard that had a big x carved deep into its bark. Whenever
something terrible or very good happened, I would go there
with my small black and white fox terrier, Izzie, and sit on the
ground with my back against the tree. Sitting alone by that tree
became my own particular way of listening. I felt peaceful
sitting there but it was years later before I got an inkling of
what God wanted me to do with my life.

While Aunt Ethel showed me the importance of listening
for God in quiet, Mama encouraged me to be gracefully
independent. She told me that when she was in kindergarten,
her father, Frank Kinney, told her he would give her a pony if
she would dare to go to school barefoot. She didn't take her
father up on his dare, but she did understand that going barefoot would make her stand out, which takes courage. She knew
he wanted her to be herself, even if people laughed at her.

My grandfather's lesson has been a touchstone for me,
because my work has often been unpopular. Like Mama when
she was in kindergarten, I have never wanted people to think I
was strange. I have often had to do battle with a voice within
me that asks, what will other people think if you do that?
Remembering Frank Kinney's challenge still encourages me.

Mother grew up in Cincinnati, Ohio, next to her grandparents, in a house surrounded by the houses of her Kinney aunts,
uncles and cousins, who all lived on properties from the original Kinney homestead. As a child, she would call to see what
her various relatives were serving for supper, then she would
decide where she would go to eat. After supper, she often
walked over to Aunt Emma's for stories. Reared in the midst of
such an easy-going extended family gave Mama a sense of
stability, which may partly explain her independent spirit.

Mama also helped me to value creativity. I was in awe as I
watched her paint a picture of my pony without even looking
at her! I tried to do the same thing, but my horse never looked
like a real horse. I used to tell Mama not to keep her paintings

*Mama with
her father,
Frank Kinney*

Arthur Pfeiffer, my maternal grand uncle

Adam Bridge, my great-grandfather, the "Crusading Editor"

in a closet below the front stairway. Though she painted for her own enjoyment, I thought her work should be on the walls of our house or in galleries where everyone could see it. I vowed never to keep my talents hidden "underneath the stairway."

One way Mother did allow her talent to show was in the beauty of our home. She worked with Tom Rather, a Houston architect, to plan our long brick house, which looked as though it had grown up with the pine trees that surrounded it. I can still see her up on a ladder in the recreation room, painting Scandinavian folk art motifs on the rafters. In my childhood bedroom, the wallpaper she chose was covered with inter-twining strawberry plants that echoed the tiny branches of a big gum tree outside my window.

While Mother encouraged my creative side, Dad showed me the value of the pragmatic. His experience as a leader in the business world and in overcoming adversity has always served as a positive model for me. In 1928, when he was twenty-two years old, his father, Charles Shartle, and his older brother's father-in-law, J.W. Link, bought the majority interest in a steel casting foundry located on Houston's eastside, which they named Texas Electric Steel Casting Company or TESCO.

Then, incredibly, they decided to make my father, who had no experience, the director. He was put in charge of experienced men twice his age. He got the company off to a good start, but then almost lost everything in the Depression. His successes encouraged me to believe I too could make plans and follow through on them.

I believe Dad wanted me to learn at an early age what he had been forced to learn in his twenties. That's why, from the time I was five years old, he devised jobs to teach me to work hard and earn money. He paid me twenty-five cents an hour to rake pine needles away from clumps of Saint Augustine grass so the sun could get through and help the grass to grow. I worked alone but never far from Dad and his helper, Marshall. Marshall

With Mama and Dad

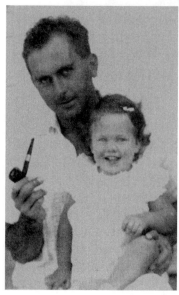

Tommy, Lenore, and me.

was stocky, short and black; Dad was tall and thin. I remember them bending over in tandem, either working on the septic tank pipes west of the house among the banana trees, or pouring kerosene in the ditches to keep the mosquitoes from hatching their eggs. As they moved from one job to the next, I moved too, so I could always keep an eye on them.

Another person who made me stretch was my big brother, Tommy, who taught me to swim and to ride. He hauled Do-si-do, my quarter horse, to Tomball, Texas, where we competed in barrel races at rodeos. Most of all, he taught me to have confidence in my own strength so that even now, when I am tempted to give up, his coaching slips in. I would swim forty lengths, and he'd be waiting at the end of the pool yelling, "Keep on, you'll get a second wind!" I knew I would, because he said so, and I always did.

Around 1975, Tommy found his joy. He bought a place in New Mexico, named it *Mountain Music Ranch*, and trained

Tommy, Lenore, Gretchen, Charles

Missouri walking horses. Just before he died of cancer, on Valentine's Day in 1987, I had been meaning to write him a letter. He died before I could write it, so I read it at his memorial service, held in Crockett, Texas:

February 14, 1987

Dear Tommy,

When you left for boarding school so long ago, it seemed you left forever. Now, you're dead, and I never had a chance to tell you how much I appreciate the time you took to teach me to be stronger than I thought I could be. I can still hear your coaching voice as you stood on the edge of the pool teaching me to swim: "Kick, kick kick kick," you'd yell.

Now, I'm yelling at you, "I love you Tommy. I really do and always will!"

Before Tommy left for Mercersburg Academy, in Pennsylvania, he taught me how to manage the chicken business, so that by the time he departed, I was able to handle it with Dad's and Marshall's help. It then became my job to buy the feed, care for the chickens, collect the eggs, and sell them. Around 1950, my younger brother, Charles, joined me in the work, which we called "our business." Although our neighbors and Mother furnished ready markets for the eggs, and Dad furnished the land, the chicken house, the nesting barrels and the chickens, still, after buying the feed, we had a hard time breaking even. While I liked being in business, the chickens were a pain. Partly tongue in cheek, I suggested to Charles, "Let's don't feed them until they start laying more eggs." Fortunately, Charles disagreed. The whole experience made me feel sympathetic to farmers and taught me to be careful about money.

Dad finally gave us a hand by helping us buy a sow that had already been bred. Remembering our struggle to pay for chicken feed, I made a deal with Mrs. Baird's Bakery to pick up their day-old bread at no cost. Carrying a big bucket, I rode my

horse bareback to nearby neighbors' houses to collect their
garbage. By mixing garbage and bread with water in barrels,
Charles and I cut down our feed bill.

When Pudgy was ready to give birth, we hauled her over to
the barnyard and into a horse stall, because we didn't want the
baby pigs to drop into the mud when they were born. I still
remember Pudgy standing up, facing the inside wall, and me in
the barnyard, with my hands on my hips at the stall door.
Dressed in my torn blue jeans and knee-high black rubber
boots, I yelled out to her as each baby dropped, "Good girl,
good girl, come on Pudgy, have another one!" I counted up the
dollars as each baby popped out. She had thirteen.

I felt like a real businesswoman! I knew we could keep on
feeding Pudgy, that she would nurse the babies, and then we
could sell them for around fifty dollars apiece. That was a big
improvement over the twenty-five cents an hour I had earned
from raking leaves, or going in the red raising chickens. Looking back, I'm grateful Dad helped me get that experience in
business early on.

In an unusual way, that farm was an apprenticeship program
for my life. I simultaneously learned to manage a business and
to be compassionate. When I was eight years old, Tommy began
teaching Marshall and me everything he had learned from the
veterinarian who came to our house. Together, Marshall and I
doctored the horses. Marshall would hold my colt while I
pulled screw worms out of her wounds with a long tweezers. I
took care of the dogs' and cats' wounds by myself. My love of
animals and experience in caring for them helped me to be
self-confident later in caring for my own newborn babies.

Working with Marshall built in me a love and respect for
people different from me. Marshall's real first name was
Theophilus, which I learned meant "love of God." Since he
never had children, and I never had a real grandfather, he
became almost like a grandfather to me. We worked in our

large vegetable garden together and helped each other with all the chores related to the animals. I remember going down to Buffalo Bayou blackberry picking with him. We laughed and joked, and he told me about "mother wit," which I later realized is a combination of love and intuition. On these excursions, he always took a big stick to protect us from copperheads and water moccasins, which frightened Marshall more than me. Some evenings when I was studying at Tommy's desk by the second-story window, facing the barn, I'd hear him call from the driveway below, "Come help me bring in the horses." I knew he could do it alone, but he wanted me to protect him from the snakes.

Though I was still shaky about being alone, in many ways I did feel grown-up. What I missed was not having ever known any of my grandparents. I so much wanted to have aunts, uncles and cousins next door, as Mama had had when she was growing up. Nevertheless, my parents made living in the country more fun by inviting interesting people from town, from Mexico and from all over the United States. I loved talking with their friends and thought of them as my imaginary family, calling many of them "aunt" and "uncle." Being with Mother and Dad as they welcomed people with such ease helped me feel connected to most everyone, including strangers.

Probably this is why I didn't hesitate to introduce myself to Booz, who had adopted her maiden name as her first name. Just before Easter when I was about nine years old, I was riding on Merry Legs, my strawberry roan pony, collecting Spanish moss to make nests for the Easter bunny. That's when I saw Booz Beach in her yard. When Booz saw me, she invited me to climb over the fence for a Dr. Pepper on ice. I tied up Merry Legs, scaled the wire fence, then pulled my fox terrier, Izzie, underneath. Booz and I sat down with her boxer dog, Wendy, and Izzie for our first of many long conversations. During hundreds of visits after that, we talked about our

Me and my quarter horse

animals and our friends, speculated about life after death, and planned what to make Mother and Dad for Christma and birthdays. Dad heard me talk so much about Booz that he made a stile, so Izzie and I could climb over the fence. Together, Booz and I started an unusual neighborhood group that eventually expanded to include our dogs, my horses, her husband, my sister, my brothers and Mother and Dad and most of their friends. No one was surprised that I named my quarter horse colt Little Booz; then Booz named her first daughter Gretchen. My horseback trips to Booz's were my first step in traveling alone and making friends with a stranger.

As much as I loved being with Booz and other grown-ups, I also had fun with friends my own age. My cousins, Martin and Mack, and I called ourselves The Gray Cat Club. We used to hide way up in the dark hayloft, the best place to look for Smokey's newest litter of kittens. Even though the hayloft was

Theophilus Marshall;
he lived in a small house near me
from the time I was 8 years old.

Bruce Keckley and Dad
at TESCO, Texas Electric
Steel Casting Company

half a mile from the house, we huddled up there and whispered our plans to spy on the grown-ups. While our parents and their friends barbecued, we used bricks left over from the construction of our house to make a fort in the first pasture among the pines. We covered it with pine needles so the Japanese couldn't spot us if they launched attacks on the United States.

In the fifth grade, my first year at St. John's Episcopal School, I started a softball team. Three of us, Betsy Murray, the catcher, whom my dad nicknamed Sour Pickles because she was always smiling, Betty Bateman, first base, and I, the pitcher, formed a club. We called ourselves The Three Musketeers until Dad renamed us "The Three Messy Steers." Betsy and Betty were, for me, the perfect balance as friends. Betsy made me laugh and Betty made me think. One drizzly Saturday, up in the hay loft, we took a cue from Tom Sawyer, pricked our fingers, made marks on papers with our blood, and promised to be loyal friends forever. We built a good team and won most of our games, even against the boys!

For me, Houston was made up of three different worlds: the outskirts where I lived, the town where I went to school and the Fifth Ward, where my dad's factory was located. Marshall was the link between where we lived and poor people in the Fifth Ward. On trips to Dad's factory, which was located outside my everyday world, I noticed the hundreds of barely livable shacks. The fact that Marshall had lived in that part of town before he worked for us made people in those shacks come alive for me.

People in the large River Oaks homes were real to me because many of them were my classmates, but sometimes, when I visited my friends in those large houses and noticed what seemed like wasteful fanciness, I felt a bit lost. Our property was so full of animals and our home so filled with people and life that, by contrast, some of those big River Oaks places with large rooms that went unused seemed lifeless. Noticing the difference between Fifth Ward and River Oaks was the first time I realized there was a big gap between poverty and wealth in the world.

I wanted to talk with my Dad about the problems of poor people, but he was mainly focused on how to make a living. Since making money was so important to him, I worried that he might be a materialist – which of course he was. Yet he was also full of fun, and to me that meant full of spirit. I knew he was a loving man, because he loved me, but sometimes I felt lonely around him. It was so hard to talk to him about things that mattered to me. I encouraged him to appreciate Mother's paintings, for example, but that seemed out of his realm. He hardly ever wanted to chat, because he had his mind on completing daily tasks. Now, I see Dad in me, in that I have always wanted to "keep on movin'" until the job is done!

During my high school years at St. John's, I often wondered what could be done about the injustices I saw in Houston. I particularly remember working with a black church in Fifth Ward to plan Easter egg hunts for the children. This kind of experience was good for us, and fun for the children, but hardly helpful for the people in that church who needed good jobs much more than Easter eggs. I knew that businessmen like Dad were helpful because they provided work, but I also knew that more needed to be done. Now, I look back and wish community service had been part of our high school curriculum. It would have been stimulating to have had discussions about the gap between wealthy and poor communities in our city and state. I wonder how we would have felt if we had known that black schools in Houston had outhouses instead of regular toilets? As long as our eyes remained shut to the realities of poverty, effective social change never would happen. Of course I didn't think in these terms then, even though I knew something was wrong.

In many ways, I was different from my classmates. I might

Mama and Dad in Crockett

have been tempted to conform more than I did if we had lived in town. Fortunately, I grew up in what was then an isolated place in the country. Being alone so much of the time gave me a chance to realize what was important to me. I was planted in a good place, with a mother and father who represented for me vision and hard work. It was there that I first learned to love and trust. That was the soil from which everything else grew. This includes my way of talking to God, my concern for justice, love of beauty, delight in quiet, knowledge of business, and ease in welcoming friends and strangers. Confidence in my ability to care for animals translated later into finding ways to help people. There, in my first home, I learned to copy my Dad's "take charge" independent style as I tromped in deep mud to care for sick horses, shoveled manure, collected the neighbors' garbage, fed the pigs, and sold eggs. When I think of it, my childhood was a combination of reality and paradise.

2

The Fabric of Kinship

My horizons expanded when I left the home I so loved. From 1955 to 1975, I was on the move. During those years, I made friends from France to India and from Japan to Mexico. I also had some experiences that made me feel closer to God. During those years, step by step, I began to feel the whole world was a part of me.

Mother had a very independent streak and always encouraged me to reach out beyond my everyday boundaries. She, who had been a traveler from the time she was seven years old, got me started. She often took a streetcar all by herself from Cincinnati, Ohio, across the river to Fort Thomas, Kentucky, to visit her relatives. She taught me that places remain sterile until we make friends there.

Before our first trip to Mexico, when I was eight years old, Mother told me to be extra polite, because Mexican people have exemplary manners. "Be sure to say, *gracias* and *por favor*," she constantly reminded me. She also encouraged me to honor their customs by wearing dresses, by appreciating their food and learning their language. Because she had encouraged me to learn some phrases, by the time we went to Mexico City I knew enough Spanish to begin making friends. When cute boys came up to chat, I'd get out my tiny dictionary and do the best I could.

When I was in the tenth grade, Mama planned a trip for my sister, my cousins, Aunt Saralee and me. We visited some of the Caribbean Islands and parts of Surinam, in South America. At dawn our first morning in Port of Spain, then the capital of Trinidad, I went up to the roof of the Queen's Park Hotel, where we were staying, and viewed the whole town. I decided to explore the area up above the city, left a note for Mama and set out. As I came to the poorer section of town, about two miles from the hotel, I saw a tall black woman walking down the hill toward me. I told her my name, and she told me hers was Josephine. I asked her if I could join her. She agreed. I liked her right away. We talked about our families. What I remember most vividly from our conversation is hearing, in answer to one of my many questions, that her whole family lived on $125 a year.

In the United States, I had not had many chances to meet people like Josephine. The fact that her family lived on such a scant amount concerned me so much that after our trip I didn't want to buy any clothes. Mother suggested that my frugality could not help people like Josephine, but that did not stop me from worrying. I realized Josephine's situation was probably true for lots of people. Later, I learned it was the reality for families in two-thirds of the world.

My experiences traveling with Mama helped prepare me to go alone to Europe. The summer after I graduated from high school, I went to France, under the auspices of *The Experiment in International Living*. This organization, as its name suggests, arranged for students to live with families in foreign countries. Experiment programs follow one basic pattern. Ten students from one country go to the same city in a foreign country, where each student stays with a different family for approximately three weeks.

Before my trip to France, I thought of people in other

countries as *foreigners*, or worse, as abstractions. I wondered what my French family would be like and how I could live with strangers who did not speak English. When I visited Aunt Ethel in Virginia on my way to the port of departure, she said, "Use sympathetic imagination. It will help your new family to accept you more easily and also will help you to feel at home with them." By *sympathetic imagination*, she meant I should imagine walking in their shoes and being aware of ways I could contribute to their lives. That same afternoon, Aunt Ethel looked at me intently with her large gray-blue eyes, smiled confidently, opened her arms and said, "You will have possibilities in your life, as wide as a vast circle. Most people only experience a tiny piece of this circle, like this," she said as she made an imaginary cut in the circle like a small piece of pie. From Aunt Ethel's, I went to Montreal where I got on the boat to France. Once on the ship, I was given a letter from Mama:

> Dearest Gretchen,
>
> Save this to read until you are on the sea and have a calm moment. Perhaps you'd better just drop it in the water, because I know that time won't come until you're about 90.
>
> If you feel a little panicky when you sail, think nothing of it. Everyone does. I still do – especially if it's at nite. Take 1/2 of a Dramamine, and say a little prayer.
>
> Some people like Uncle Willard [Aunt Ethel's husband] think I'm a little crazy to let you do this. They say you'll become too sophisticated and lose your charm, but I think knowledge and experience never hurt anyone who thinks fundamentally right.
>
> God bless you and the very "bonnest" of voyages.
>
> Mother

Thirty-five years later when I came across this letter, I cried. It was so like Mother always to encourage me to explore. The fact that she trusted me so completely boosted my self-confidence.

Aunt Ethel and Mama

My visit with Aunt Ethel and Mama's note got me off to a good start, and I did have the "bonnest" of voyages!

I arrived in France on Bastille Day, July 14th, 1955. That very first night, I somehow got separated from my group which was a blessing in disguise because it gave me a chance to enjoy my first French supper alone in a Parisian sidewalk café. There, I met a French couple, who invited me to join them. When they heard I was from Texas, they asked about cowboys, Indians, and oil wells, then told me about the Texas paratroopers who had saved their town toward the end of the war. They were so grateful. After dinner, they kindly drove me to my hotel.

My host family, the Ditners, lived in an apartment in Colmar, a town in Alsace-Lorraine near the German border. I loved spending long periods of time around the table during and after lunch. I felt honored that they all paid so much attention to my stories, told in halting French, and I listened carefully as they told me what they had done that day and then we all talked about world events.

Madame Ditner was like a good mother to me. We biked to the market and sometimes visited the cathedral on the way, where she taught me the rudiments of Gothic architecture. On our trips to the country, we would stop in small cafés for lunch, and again later for tea. My friendship with her and her children has continued to this day and has been handed down to my own children.

One reason the Ditners welcomed me so readily was because of the generosity of American soldiers who had been there ten years earlier. "It was the Americans," Madame Ditner told me, "who freed my father from the German prison camp." She said that when her mother saw him walking back home after the war, he was so emaciated she did not recognize him. He died soon afterwards.

Even though many French people understandably resented the Germans, I admired the efforts made by the people in both countries to forget about their animosities once the war had ended. Groups of French women volunteered to work with Germans in rebuilding some of their bombed cities. I heard that both Alsatians and Germans exchanged students shortly after the war.

Mother and Dad met me at the ship when I returned from France, then drove me to Wellesley. I chose Wellesley for the natural beauty of the campus and for its excellence, because I wanted to be well prepared for my life work – whatever that might be. I chose the hardest courses partly to challenge myself and because I wanted to learn more about the TRUTH in order to become clear about what I was to do with my life. I pushed myself to focus only on the academic, yet the more I looked into the realm of abstractions for real answers, the more frustrated I became. It finally dawned on me that the kind of truth I was looking for was not an abstract entity that could be separated from real life.

Wellesley was beautiful. The professors were challenging, but it was not fun. I missed the warmth of home and my friends, and the congeniality of St. John's School. In a word I was lonely.

I was so glad to spend the summer at home after my freshman year, working with real life challenges as recreation director at DePelchin Faith Home. My job was planning daytime programs for thirty orphans from ages five to nineteen years old. That was too much for me to handle by myself, so several friends helped out by taking the orphans hiking and by giving them cooking and tennis lessons. I invited the children to our pool to teach them to swim. After I went back to Wellesley that fall, I heard that the oldest group had won a swimming championship in Houston!

The satisfaction I had that summer should have been a good sign to me, but I didn't know it then. Perhaps I was expecting a conclusive "aha!" kind of moment that would tell me what to do with my life. Maybe I was looking so hard I didn't notice the clues.

Back at Wellesley for my sophomore year, I was again immersed in my courses. My favorite teacher was my Biblical History professor, Fred Denbeaux. From him, I learned that one could be intelligent and still have faith. I only wish he had balanced his emphasis on faith with the importance of loving our neighbors, strangers as well as people who live nearby. As far as I can remember, he never talked about what Jesus meant by neighbor. As I see now, and as Jesus said when he spoke about the first and second commandments, loving one's neighbor and loving God are inseparable. Mark's gospel tells us:

> One of the scribes came near, and he asked him, "which commandment is the first of all?"

> Jesus answered, "The first is, hear, O Israel: the Lord our God, the Lord is one;

> you shall love the Lord your God with all your heart, with all your soul, with all your mind, and with all your strength.

> The second is this, You shall love your neighbor as yourself. There is no greater commandment than these."

> (Mark 12: 28-31)

It would have been helpful if I had been led to connect Bible readings like this one to my own experiences with neighbors – both my new neighbors in a foreign country and "distant neighbors" like the children at Faith Home in Houston, whose world was different from my own. Then I might have realized that even while I was searching for a direction in my life, I was already on the right track.

For Mr. Denbeaux, believing in the resurrection was central to being a Christian. Ever since I was a little girl and buried that tiny dead chick, I had wanted so much to believe in the resurrection. At Wellesley, I was coping with a dilemma of faith in the most academic, scientific environment I had ever known. At 8:30 a.m. in biology class, Dr. Bull taught us never to trust any data without valid proof. At 11 a.m., in Biblical History, Mr. Denbeaux explained that a person who does not have faith in the resurrection is not a Christian.

One afternoon, I sat in my room and beat my desk with my fist after hearing Mr. Denbeaux talk about the resurrection. I said to myself, "I want to believe it, but where is the proof?" To know Jesus had risen might mean that – in some miraculous way – he could be with us now. When I tried to discuss my feelings with Sarah Dailey, my Unitarian roommate, she said, "Gretchen, that makes absolutely no sense. It would be irrational to believe in that." Her detachment stood in sharp contrast to my passion.

The following year, in 1957, Sarah and I decided to study in Paris with the *Sweet Briar Junior Year Abroad* program. While we were there, a French friend invited me to join ten thousand students on a pilgrimage organized by the Catholic Church. We were to walk from the outskirts of Paris to Chartres Cathedral on the Saturday before Easter. We walked three abreast singing pilgrimage songs and talking about the meaning of the Trinity. Since I knew practically nothing about the theology of the Catholic Church, I asked lots of questions. By the time we got to Chartres, I felt close to my new friends and also closer to God. Sunday afternoon, thousands of us were singing as we entered the town of Chartres and then again inside the cathedral. The beauty of the cathedral, combined with my new friends' kindness brought me to tears. I let myself be open to faith. It was like allowing myself to fall. I realized: this is what faith feels like. I can believe even when I don't have proof. I felt ready to commit myself to becoming a Catholic on the spot.

However, I found no way to explore these new stirrings that spring before I left Paris. Even if I had, the Catholic Church back then might have been too confining for me. Also, I had begun to admire Gandhi in high school and it had vaguely occurred to me that I should at least explore Hinduism before committing myself to Christianity. My sophomore course with Mr. Denbeaux answered some of my questions about faith, but his exclusive approach to Jesus and intense focus on the resurrection made me edgy. That's why the seeds planted during the pilgrimage to Chartres in 1958 lay waiting until years later to take root.

I felt more at home my senior year at Wellesley. That's when I met Surrendra Paul, a thin, dark, handsome man, who was a student at M.I.T. from Calcutta. He was happy-go-lucky, not the type with whom I wanted to discuss my religious quest. Even though I hardly ever talked to Surrendra about my serious questions, our common dream to gather people from different countries brought us together. We called our work "bridge-building." I invited M.I.T. students to Wellesley to visit classes, take walks around the lake and discuss ideas. Surrendra, who had three telephones going all at once, planned big international dances at M.I.T. He would tell me about the M.I.T. male students, then I would match them with American Wellesley women if they were foreign or vice versa.

Surrendra's style was different from mine. He was not at all embarrassed about having fancy parties or riding around in a big black chauffeur-driven car. In India, people revered *Ganesha*, the elephant god to whom one prayed for money. For me, God and money were antithetical. I would not have liked driving around in a fancy black car, even if I could have. I never even hinted to my friends that my family had money, partly because I didn't want that fact to separate me from others. I felt so uneasy dealing with money, I tried to ignore the whole issue.

In the midst of trying to ignore money, I didn't thank Dad enough for paying my St. John's and Wellesley tuitions. I took those gifts too much for granted. While my own responsibilities, like clothes and trips were smaller in scale than Dad's, they worried me more, because I paid for them from my seventy-five dollar per month allowance. Because of the simple way I dressed, some friends at Wellesley asked me if I were on a scholarship, which pleased me since I never wanted to be labeled a wealthy Texan.

On at least one occasion, I carried these feelings too far. The day I graduated from Wellesley, in 1959, I hurt Mother's feelings. She gave me a ring she had had made for me by using three tiny diamonds from her own mother's engagement ring. Instead of telling her how grateful I was, I told her that I never planned to wear either diamonds or furs. Fortunately, Aunt Ethel was nearby. She took me aside, looked into my eyes and said, "Gretchen, you are not from a poor family. It is important to be grateful for your heritage and to accept who you are." When my ring was stolen the very next year while in Indonesia, I was distressed, remembering what Aunt Ethel had said.

The year after I graduated, I completed my academic work for a master's degree in French Literature. While I was studying French at the University of Houston, I invented a direct method for teaching French to elementary school children. I spoke only French with the children from the beginning so they would begin to think in French. The five, six and seven year old children were so surprised to sit on the floor in a circle with their teacher and listen to stories in a "secret" language, that they learned without trying. One might say it's not possible to be in love with a whole group of children at once, but that's how it felt to me.

While I was happily engaged in this work, Mother and Dad invited me to join them on a trip around the world to begin in the fall of 1960. On our trip, we were to visit Jerusalem, Teheran, Afghanistan, New Delhi, Bombay, Mysore in south India, Ceylon, Calcutta, Burma, Cambodia, Hong Kong, and Japan. My way of traveling was different from that of my parents, in that I preferred to stay with families and to take buses instead of private transportation.

At the beginning of the trip, when we were staying in the Ashoka Hotel in New Delhi, I told Mother that I felt uneasy staying with other tourists in luxury, walled off from the Indian people. I got scared about my future when I imagined my whole life being consumed by jumping from one thing to the next, symbolized those days by moving from hotel to hotel. I wanted to accomplish something real. I liked building international understanding, but my dreams were big and unspecific. Mother listened as I brainstormed, and suggested that I be patient.

Minutes after we arrived in Ceylon (present day Sri Lanka), I was paged in the dining room. "Trunk call from Calcutta for Gretchen Shartle." It was Surrendra inviting me to come to Calcutta for a party that was to include industrialists from Poland and other Eastern Block countries. Of course I wanted to go! During my flight, I read *The Soul of India*, by Amaury de Riencourt. That's how I learned about *Shantiniketan*, an international university founded by the statesman and poet, Rabindranath Tagore. It was located in rural Bengal, about two hours from Calcutta.

At Surrendra's party, I felt completely at home, meeting people from India as well as Czechoslovakia, Poland and Yugoslavia. What impressed me most were all the different kinds of food covering his long dining room table. I kept tasting one dish after another expecting to find meat, but everything was completely vegetarian. The day after the party, I took a train to the small town of Bolpur near Shantiniketan, (the name means "place of peace."), I found I could take courses in Indian History, Ancient Indian Literature and Religion, all given in English.

A few days later, when Mother, Dad, and my brother Charles arrived in Calcutta, I surprised them with the news that I planned to stay in India and study for a few months. Dad was opposed to my plan. Since I had never before gone against him,

I was so anxious that my whole body broke out in hives! In the spirit of her own father's "barefoot pony dare," Mother backed me up. I held firm and stayed.

Shantiniketan was a dream come true. I rented a room in the small building called Scholars' Block. Tagore liked the simple life, which appealed to me too. We slept on board beds and had Indian style showers at noon, ice-cold water dipped in large tin cups from a barrel. I sang as I cooked my breakfast and supper on a small two-burner stove in my room, celebrating the victory of feeling at home, by myself, in India. That was a far greater challenge than living in France.

What I particularly liked about Shantiniketan was that I was an insider. I felt privileged to join the other students for lunch in a place called "the kitchen," a low dark room separated into four sections: vegetarian girls, vegetarian boys, non-vegetarian boys and non-vegetarian girls. I sat in the section with the vegetarian girls. Every meal was the same: rice, mashed lentils, a cauliflower-and-potato mixture cooked in a horrible smelling mustard oil and yogurt. The girls shoveled the food out of buckets onto copper plates and bowls, and we ate with our hands. Eating with my right hand seemed strange at first, but I came to like it.

It was a joy to be part of the scene, listening when the Shantal people passed by my room playing their flutes as they went to and from their work in the rice fields. Then, when I rode home on my bike, dressed in my long red cotton sari, a group of children would yell, "Gita-di, Gita-di." Gita was their Indian name for me, and di means sister. They would catch my hand and run along, singing together with me all the way back to my room at the Scholars' Block.

One of the highlights of my time at Shantiniketan was getting to know Motoo Yamagiwa, a young Japanese writer. He was writing a book on Ashoka, a third century BC Indian emperor who modeled the best ideals of Indian culture, especially its reverence for all life. Ashoka, even after abandoning aggressive warfare, still managed to expand the territories under his jurisdiction by enlisting the "dharma" (doctrine of righteousness). Ashoka, like Gandhi later, strongly adhered to "ahimsa" (non-injury to human beings or animals).

Following my own Ashoka-like aspirations, I decided to help Motoo learn English and to be his first American friend. I saw this as one small way I could help prevent wars. As I got to know him, I realized that when World War II broke out, if I had one friend like him, I would have been against that war. Neither Motoo nor I had known anyone from the other's country before we met.

Paradoxically, the first thing that brought us together was the Second World War. Having lived through Pearl Harbor and a war in which I felt our country had been wronged, I was surprised to see that his antagonism toward Americans was even stronger than mine toward the Japanese people. One of the first things he told me in pantomime and hesitant English was about a visit that he made to downtown Tokyo during the war. He was horrified to discover masses of dead people, lying like broken mannequins in the streets after a U.S. bombing raid. As I spent time getting to know Motoo, I was so focused on softening his attitude toward the United States that I didn't notice my feelings about him and the Japanese people were changing. As he was becoming my friend, I began to drop my unexamined stereotypes of the Japanese.

My life was filled with experiences that combined the personal and the global. Motoo and I were not only friends, but together we represented two countries that had been at war less than a generation earlier. My friendship with Motoo led me to believe I could have an impact on the international scene by making friends. With these thoughts in mind, shortly before I left Shantiniketan I decided to take a nineteen-hour train ride to Allahabad to attend a Winter School for foreign students. A highlight for me there was getting to know Marina and Alex Plechov from a language school in Moscow. Since like me, they were foreigners in India, and since they spoke English quite well, I had more in common with them than with many Indian students. Also, the cold war was already poisoning our atmosphere, and I wanted to do everything possible to break through the walls of mistrust building between our countries.

Just before we left Allahabad, I was asked to act as the American representative and Alex Plechov was asked to be the representative for Russia in an official citywide ceremony with the mayor. While I was limited to English, Alex thanked the mayor in Hindi. Right then, I promised myself to learn Hindi. My competitive spirit had come to the fore, and as a good American, I did not want Alex's country to outshine mine. All three of us were committed to our different nationalities, but we had become very good friends and I hated to say good-bye.

Then something puzzling happened the very next week, when I was visiting Surrendra's family in Calcutta. One afternoon, Surrendra and I had lunch at the Park Hotel in downtown Calcutta and, as we were going down the wide hotel stairway, I saw Marina and Alex Plechov coming up. They were leading a group of Russians. When I tried to greet them, they pretended not to know me. I was troubled because I genuinely liked them, and I had hoped that together we might have had a positive influence, however tiny, on the world scene. For a brief moment, I wished Surrendra might bring us back together. After all, India was not aligned with either the east or the west. But the moment passed so quickly that neither of us was able to think of a good response. I was angry and frustrated that my dream of building peace through friendships had been superseded by the Plechov's loyalty to their country or perhaps their fear of what would happen to them if they spoke to me. For years after that, I tried without success to contact them at their language school in Moscow.

During that same visit in Calcutta, Surrendra took me to visit his family's steel factory, which was his particular responsibility. I was amazed to see lots of cows standing in the muddy street, just outside the front door of his plant. As we made our way through the crowds and beggars, past the animals that messed up not only the streets but many of the temples in Calcutta, I sometimes longed for the quiet of western churches and the Texas woods.

During those times, it helped me to remember the Sanskrit prayer we had heard every week in the Brahmo Samaj service at Shantiniketan: "Om, the god that pervades the world, is replete in all the beings of this world." The prayer reminded me that there was a connection between the animals cluttering the streets and the Hindus' respect for all life. The Hindu people's reverence for life was also evident in the political arena. Prime Minister Nehru's policy of non-alignment with both the eastern and western blocs was consistent with the ancient tradition of *ahimsa* or nonviolence, which resonated in every aspect of Indian life, from their vegetarian ways to their refusal to become engaged in wars.

Sometimes I considered living in India, partly because I wanted to help out and also because I had become so attracted to it. But then I thought of the American women I had seen who lived there. It seemed to me that most of them had lost their identity. They worshipped Indian gods, wore saris and seemed lost. Seeing them, clarified for me that while I was attracted to India, my roots were in the United States. My vitality, I knew, came from being closely connected to my family and my own country. It seemed the wisest way for me to give both to India and to the United States was to learn in depth about Indian life and culture so I could teach in the United States about South Asia.

When I got ready to leave India, Surrendra's family loaded me

Shantal farmers working in the rice fields

A typical class at Shantiniketan

A party at Surrenda's home in Calcutta: from the left, me, Surrendra's brother-in-law, a European guest, and Surrendra

The mother of Mishtani, my best friend at Shantiniketan

with gifts as a farewell sign of their love. They had already given me so much by opening their home to me that I felt overwhelmed, but I had learned that receiving is another way of giving. In January 1961, I said good-bye with a full heart, then headed off alone with tickets to Thailand, Cambodia, Vietnam, and Japan. The observations I made in India, added to the growing violence I saw in Saigon, confirmed my decision to teach about Asia in American schools.

After five days in Saigon, I left Vietnam and flew to Tokyo, where Motoo surprised me at the airport. When I told Motoo good-bye in India, I did not expect to see him again. After making plans with him to travel to Kyushu together, I went by train to Kyoto. There I spent a week with the Ohigashi family, whose name had been given to me by the *Experiment in International Living*. That night in February 1961 when I arrived at their home, the moon was just bright enough so I could see the river. I first saw Ikuchan in that moonlight.

Ikuchan Ohigashi was a fifteen year-old, rosy-cheeked girl who became my best friend during my stay there. When she and I visited the rock garden in Ryongen, she said in her sing-song voice, "It makes my heart move." Her comment made my heart move, too. All the Ohigashis could speak some English, except for the grandmother and Mrs. Ohigashi, and we communicated through gestures. The combination of feeling at home with the Ohigashi family, finding how dearly I cared for Ikuchan, and seeing the beauty of the gardens, palaces, and Japanese inns – all this opened my heart to the Japanese people.

In mid-February, Motoo and I set off by train for Miyazaki, on the island of Kyushu in southern Japan. When we arrived, we met a friend of Motoo's uncle, who made arrangements for us to stay and work with a four-generation family who all lived and worked together on their farm. Mr. and Mrs. Kawano, Mr. Kawano's mother, their son and daughter-in-law and tiny six-month old grandchild, all met us at the door of their home,

Dr. and Mrs. Ohigashi, my hosts in Kyoto

kneeling down and bowing with their hands in front of them. We made friends fairly easily as we sat around their open fire eating toasted mushrooms and drinking hot green tea.

That night, we all let the mistrust from the past drop away, even though only a little over fifteen years before, I had had no trouble calling the Japanese people "Japs." Their nation had bombed Pearl Harbor, and ours had dropped atom bombs on Hiroshima and Nagasaki. These things were unspoken, but were still in the air even as we were laughing together at the table. I hoped our friendship would be an antidote against future wars.

When I got up at six the next morning, I was surprised to see Mr. Kawano sitting by the fire practicing *Zee Stars at Night,* which I taught him the evening before. Later, when Motoo appeared, we both asked Mr. Kawano for permission to help in the fields that morning. Kawanosan was planting one third of his land, or two and one half acres, in pine trees so he could sell the lumber in twenty years. We joined the women who were poking sliced pine branches into dirt that had been hoed, then followed them in a line, stamping the ground down tight.

Dressed in my version of a Japanese peasant woman's costume – that is, in moccasins, five sweaters and "mompe," (full long patterned cotton pants like theirs), I hoped to blend in. In spite of my Japanese costume, people stopped on the road, their brown eyes large in wonder. We stamped, as they taught us a Japanese song and we taught them "You Are My Sunshine." Reluctantly, we said good-bye to the Kawano family and headed back via buses and trains to Tokyo.

Soon after Motoo and I left Kyushu in late February of 1961, I became overwhelmed with sadness, because I knew I would soon need to say good-bye to Motoo and leave Japan. He had fallen in love with me, and I was dismayed to realize I was also falling in love with him. It scared me to think of marrying a Japanese man so soon after World War II. I could not imagine taking him back to Houston where anti-Japanese feeling had not subsided.

When we returned to Tokyo, something happened that made it easier for me to leave. Three days before my flight, Motoo invited me to attend an East Asian writers' conference in Tokyo. At that conference, Motoo didn't even ask questions when some of the leaders said that U.S. soldiers in Cambodia had put babies in sacks, then thrown them in a river where they were left to drown. I was furious when he joined others in singing anti-American songs. While I did not want to say good-bye forever, I knew it would never work to marry him. In the Tokyo airport, I said good-bye to the man I loved, whom I knew I would never ever see again.

When I got home and told Mother about Motoo and how much I missed him, she said, "Gretchen, it is your decision. I can only tell you that marriage is hard enough with people from the same culture, but even harder when your backgrounds are completely different." She was wise not to have reacted more strongly. I knew she would have been supportive if I had decided to marry Motoo, but Dad would not have been pleased.

As I mourned my loss of Motoo, I searched for ways to reconnect with the joy I had felt at Shantiniketan. After so many months on the move, I was grateful for a period of quiet at our family place in the piney woods of east Texas. That summer of 1961 helped me learn a lesson I've tried never to forget, which is the importance of balancing my life between periods of activity, which I call the "outer journey," and periods of relative quiet, or the "journey inward." Whenever I've been tempted to go too much in one direction or the other, my strength has ebbed away.

After that lovely summer in 1961, spent mostly alone, I felt ready to begin the South Asian Studies Program at the University of Pennsylvania, in Philadelphia. In the fall of 1961, I began my courses in the history, art, and religions of the South Asian continent. I even learned to speak Hindi and to write the Deva Nagri script.

In 1962, I returned to India for what turned out to be a difficult trip. *The Experiment in International Living* had asked me to be an assistant leader in India. I felt honored because they told me that at age twenty-five I would be the youngest person serving in a leadership role in Asia. Without a worry, I went off to India again to accomplish my task, which was to help a group of American teachers and students adapt to their families in Ahmedabad, in the state of Gujerat in west central India. I was not as good a model as I had hoped to be, because I didn't like my own host. His wife and two boys were nice, but seldom home. The more I tried to like my host, the less I succeeded. I could not persuade him to leave me alone even for a moment. To be by myself, I used to climb up onto the roof of his house after supper, where I could see the stars and enjoy the quiet. This summer experience made it hard for me to engage enthusiastically in my academic work when I returned to the university in the fall. I was afraid it might make me cynical. Fortunately, it didn't.

Once I got my feet back on the ground at the university, five other graduate students and I initiated a mini South Asian Studies' program for high school students in the Philadelphia area. Following *The Experiment* model of national and ethnic balance, three of us were from the United States and three from India. Always working in teams of two, one an American, and one a South Asian, we gave mini-courses illustrated with slides, which focused on the economics, social structure, history and religions of South Asia.

I completed the academic requirements for my degree in 1964 and my thesis the next year. My goal was to teach in the United States about India. I wanted to let people know that everyone in the huge population of India was a sacred person

... just like any of us. I hoped to touch the hearts and minds of Americans here, as my own heart had been touched over and over again in India.

During those years of focusing on Asia, I had thought that sharing experiences and teaching about the culture of South Asia would be the way for me to awaken others. Instead, I was the one who woke up. I realized I was related to people everywhere. That feeling of kinship extended later to people in Central America whom I had never met. I believe it was those early experiences that prepared me to care deeply later, when I learned that Central America's people were suffering as victims of the policies of my own government.

3

Distant Neighbors

I met my husband-to-be, Hilbert Sabin, when I was in the midst of completing my master's degree at the University of Pennsylvania. He had come from Dickinson College in Carlisle, Pennsylvania, where he was teaching art history, to attend a meeting of South Asian scholars in Philadelphia. I found it intriguing that a painter and professor of art history would get involved in India. He introduced himself to me when I entered the lecture room. He told me later that he was smitten when he first saw me, a ruddy-cheeked, dark-haired, blue-eyed young woman dressed in a bright yellow suit. I too was swept off my feet. He was a tall, rather handsome man with a deep voice. He had a probing mind as well as a sensitive imagination that showed later in the lovely watercolors he painted on Japanese rice paper. I was glad he was preparing for a trip to India the following summer, a trip sponsored by the Ford Foundation that would pay him to do photographic studies of Hindu temple sculpture. At times I wished he would show some interest in the Peace Corps or some other aspect of altruistic service, but I had fallen in love and I decided to marry him. We married in the spring of 1964. I soon became pregnant with Kyria, then we set off for India. It was my third trip.

Over several years, I had come to realize that the number

one problem in India was overpopulation. At that time, India had over four hundred million people on a land mass much smaller than the United States. It was clear to me that India desperately needed a first rate family planning program, a view that was just beginning to be popular in India. When Hib and I went to Madras, I arranged to meet with the state family planning officer there. She told me that many women, determined to terminate their pregnancies, inserted a poisonous stick into their vaginas. If they didn't come for treatment fast enough, they died. In smaller villages, women who wanted to stop having children sometimes sought the help of the local barber and his wife. I was horrified to think of some mothers dying and of many unwanted children being born into poverty.

The following week when we visited an American friend at a missionary school in the state of Mysore, I asked one of the teachers from his school to go with me to meet the village barber and his wife. Most people in the rural areas had never heard of birth control, and I knew it was taboo for a woman, especially a foreigner like me, to mention this subject.

My American host tried to dissuade me from mentioning anything about a woman's reproductive system to the village barber, but I was determined to do what I could to help. The teacher translated as I dared to ask the barber if the women in his village would be interested in contraception. He surprised me when he said, "If you know of any way to prevent women from having children, you are an angel from God!" He agreed to be in touch with the state family-planning officer in Madras, who had told me she would help anyone I found who was receptive. I told the barber how to contact her and also wrote to give her his address. While I knew it was impossible for me to plan effective interventions anywhere as long as I was on the move, I could not resist lending a hand to the people in that one village.

After we returned to Carlisle that fall, I thought a lot about

A village barber in India

Gretchen Reading to Kyria

our baby and was concerned that my interest in world problems might conflict with being a mother. My worries subsided the minute I saw Kyria's immense blue-green eyes. As I held her warm body close to mine and nursed her, I remembered mothers in Asia and Mexico whom I had seen nursing their little ones. After so much time travelling, it was good to stay home with Kyria and with Mama, who had come for a long visit.

My husband's time for a sabbatical came when Kyria was nine months old. We decided to go to Houston to live near Mother and Dad. Hib planned to spend his days painting, and I wanted to teach school. There were no job openings in Asian Studies, so I accepted a position teaching French at Texas Southern, a university for blacks. Because Dad had been critical of the Civil Rights movement in the South, I wondered if he would be opposed to my job. He was so completely against Martin Luther King's movement that when our Unitarian minister chose to join the Selma march, Dad left the First Unitarian Church. I was sensitive to his feelings during my year at Texas Southern and didn't talk to him about my job. In turn, he never once questioned me about it.

That year, I learned more about my own inadequacies. During the early '60's, I had been so riveted on India, marriage, and Kyria that I had spent little time finding out about the struggles of black people in my own country. So, when the Ditners in France asked me about the horrors in the southern United States that they were reading about, I told them the news accounts were probably exaggerated. Then I found that groups in the South had been cursing, brutalizing, even lynching blacks. I also learned from one of my students at Texas Southern that the public school he went to in Houston in the late '50's had outhouses instead of indoor toilets. The meager facilities in their schools were matched by their inadequate academic preparation. This made it hard for them to learn French or any other foreign language.

After we left Houston and went back to Carlisle, in 1966, I attended a Community Action Planning meeting that challenged us to reach out to our communities. My friend Ida Forbis and I began a Head Start program, which we named *So Big*. A black minister offered to house the program in the local Baptist church, which made sense because most of the families in the program belonged to that church. When I was on the phone dealing with Head Start matters, Kyria would pull at my dress to get me to play with her. I tried to pay attention to her needs while I simultaneously worked on the details of starting the new program. In June 1967, the doors of the first Head Start program in Carlisle opened.

Greta was born in 1968, and I was so happy to have a new baby that part of me envied my grandmother Shartle, who had had thirteen! I was not Lucy Christine Shartle, however, and probably not the type to have thirteen babies. With two, it was already a challenge to take on anything away from home. I sensed those were the most important years of child rearing, and I was concerned about leaving Greta when she was little. When she was a year old, Kyria used to go with me to prekindergarten at Harrisburg Academy, where I taught Asian Studies to ninth and tenth graders for half a day, three times a week. At first I worried about not being with Greta but I relaxed when I noticed that she was laughing when we left and still happy when we returned.

One of my ninth-grade students at the Academy asked me if people in India grieved over dying friends and relatives as much as we do here. I think my student was really asking if those people's lives were worth as much as ours. This was in 1967, during the Vietnam War, a time when we saw people shot right in front of us on our television screens. From what we were seeing, it seemed that some Americans believed the lives of Asian people were not worth much. To answer her question, we all read *Nectar in a Sieve*, a novel by Kamala Markandaya. The excruciating pain the mother in this novel expresses when her children die was what I imagined I would feel if either Kyria or Greta died.

India was so far away, the distance between it and my life as the mother of two little children in the United States was becoming too big a stretch for me. I could not keep on teaching about India without going there at least every other year to renew my commitment. This was a terrible dilemma. I did not want to leave Kyria and Greta, nor did I feel it was wise to expose them to the unsanitary conditions in India. Also, the trip was long and expensive. My answer came late one summer night in 1969 in Crockett, Texas. After I put Kyria and Greta to bed, I took a walk down the dirt road leading to my parents' ranch house. Then I lay down in the middle of that red dirt road, looked up at the stars, and decided to relinquish India. While I let India go, I never forgot about the two-thirds world she represented to me. She had come to symbolize "distant neighbors" everywhere.

My decision to relinquish my commitment to India left me free to go with my family to Mexico. In 1970, Hib decided to spend his sabbatical there. He planned to paint, and I thought it would be an opportunity for the children to learn Spanish and get to know a different culture. Since birth, Kyria and Greta had gone to sleep hearing me sing lullabies in Spanish, French, Hindi, and Japanese. Then, as they were learning to talk, I made up songs in Spanish to teach them every-day words like "Buenos días, buenos días, cómo está? Cómo está? Muy bien gracias, muy bien gracias, dan, dan, dan," to the tune of "Frère Jacques." When Greta was two and Kyria was five and we set off for Mexico, the children were familiar with sounds of the Spanish language, though they had never wanted to speak Spanish while we were in the States.

We arrived in San Miguel de Allende just before school

started. Greta was too little to go to school, but we enrolled Kyria in a Catholic parochial school called *Fray Pedro de Gante*. I was a bit concerned, because she was the only American in the whole school, and no one in her school spoke English. Fortunately, she learned Spanish right away, partly in school and partly from the neighborhood children who invited her to jump rope with them every afternoon in the street near our house. The kids jumped and yelled out rhymes to match the rhythm of their jumps. I was relieved when, after a few weeks, Kyria was the one throwing the rope and yelling out rhymes as others jumped. Greta then joined in the street games so that later, when she started school, she was a whiz at Spanish.

Mexico was good for our family. Both children had become bilingual. Hib concentrated on his painting, and we all got involved with the community. We had also been blessed with a wonderful helper, María. While I had often felt overwhelmed with daily tasks in the U.S., life in Mexico, with María's help, was a delight. On the eve of our departure, she cried when we took her out for a farewell dinner and gave her a bright red rebozo to express our thanks. At dawn when we finished packing up the station wagon with all our belongings including Mic Mac, our dog, María was the only one there to say good-bye.

Then Hib decided to take another year off from teaching, which meant we could return to San Miguel after spending six months in the States. The second time, we rented a different house, closer to the main square. Even before unpacking the car, we went up to the house we had rented the year before, expecting to find María still working there. Hib put Greta on his back with her legs straddling his neck. As I climbed up that steep hill holding Kyria's hand, I saw María in my mind's eye, laughing as she ran down after little Greta, who had escaped into the street naked one day the year before. We were all anticipating how much fun it would be to surprise her. When we knocked on the door, nobody came. The shutters were locked. Finally, someone passed by and said, "Haven't you heard? María's dead." We went down the street to where she had lived with her children. No one was there. Then a neighbor told us that her daughter and son were living with her good friend Emilia, the superintendent of the women's jail.

Emilia explained to us that when María was at Taboada, a resort outside of town, her ex-husband killed her, perhaps because he was jealous, and she was found floating in the swimming pool. Since there was no one to bury her, her body was taken on a garbage truck to the city dump. She had been thrown out like junk. María, the person whom we paid, was the one we knew best. She was the person we trusted and counted on.

From the very beginning of my life in the U.S. and in Mexico, the people who worked for us – including their families – often became like members of our family. They also were my teachers, people who served as bridges linking me to other people I would later seek to help. Years later, when I heard of other women, women I would never meet, being killed in Central America, I thought of María. My experience of María's death later motivated me to do what I could to stop the violence in Central America.

During this second sojourn in San Miguel, we lived in the center of town near the cathedral, the orphanage, the market, the children's school, and the women's and men's jails. We often visited María's children at the women's jail, which was only two blocks from where we lived. On cold mornings, Kyria and Greta sometimes took hot cereal to the women in jail, and that's how we got to know one of the women, who was a graduate of Wellesley. This woman whose name I can not recall, had landed in jail as a result of a conflict with the mayor. Because she had no writing paper, she wrote him a long letter on toilet paper to explain her concern about some orchard trees

Kyria, age 9, with Emilia, the superintendent of the women's jail; after Maria was killed, Emilia cared for her children.

Greta, the animator in front and Kyria, the dancer in back

Our house in San Miguel

Our street in San Miguel

in a city park that she said were being needlessly destroyed.

When she discovered that the men slept on cement floors in their jail, she asked us to bring her some needles, heavy thread and lots of newspapers, which we did. She then persuaded other women prisoners to help her make newspaper mats which we delivered to the men's jail. She reminded me of our Wellesley motto: *Non Ministrari sed Ministrare*, not to be ministered unto, but to minister. The Mexican government wanted to send her back to the United States. She refused to go but they forced her to leave. Being involved with María's children and the women prisoners expanded our lives more than any school experiences in the United States could have.

Even so, I yearned for a more stimulating academic environment for my own and other children in San Miguel. After a few months of teaching English to Kyria's third-grade class, in a room where the children could barely squeeze through the chairs and desks to the blackboard, I came up with an idea to start a school for Mexican and American children in San Miguel. As I began to conceive of the possibility of a bilingual school that would include community involvement as part of the curriculum, I thought about how my own children were flourishing and realized it would benefit us to spend a few more years living in Mexico. My inspiration coincided precisely with my husband's decision to leave his teaching job at Dickinson College.

We bought a small two-bedroom house near the cathedral, next door to the Morales family. David Morales was a teacher in a local public school. His wife, Anna, was a nurse. They lived with their four children all together in one room. Elia, their beautiful bright daughter, who has since become an architect, was born exactly the same day and year as Kyria. My girls played with the Morales children a lot, and I talked with David about my hopes to start a new school. With that dream in mind, when we went back to Houston for the six month period required for the renewal of our visas, I looked for someone at the University of Houston's Department of Edcation who might help us start the school.

Dr. Stewart North agreed to come to San Miguel in the spring of 1973 to assist us. In the meantime, I talked with American and Mexican families in San Miguel and found that many were interested enough to consider enrolling their children in a bilingual school. Several of us worked from spring through the summer. We named the school after the famous Mexican minister of education José Vasconcelos, and publicized it as a bicultural, bilingual, activity-oriented elementary school. We announced the opening with posters and even asked some future students like Kyria to advertise it on the San Miguel radio. Dr. North sent down three trained teachers that September, which made it possible for us to include the American as well as the Mexican curriculum. Around thirty-five American and Mexican students signed up, and the school opened on time that fall. During the years after I left San Miguel, our tiny school grew to include two hundred and fifty students and now extends from kindergarten through high school.

The school was not my only project. Through my mother, I learned about Casa Hogar, the orphanage in San Miguel. When she visited us, Mother met one of the nuns from the orphanage on the bus from Mexico City. When the nun told her they desperately needed support, Mother suggested me. During my first visit to Casa Hogar, I learned that the children's diets were completely inadequate. That's when I got the idea to persuade a few acquaintances in the "mercado" to give their day-old food to the nuns for the orphans. Before holidays, I bought art materials and Kyria and Greta joined the children at the orphanage in making piñatas for Christmas and other celebrations.

What was unique for our family about living in San Miguel was that there we had opportunities to be involved together in community projects. Just as my Dad and my older brother made the place where we lived in the country like a business apprenticeship program for me, Hib and I aimed to provide a community training ground for our children in Mexico. Dad gave me a chance to learn about handling a business, and we gave our children the chance to feel at home in a culture different from our own.

What some people might have seen as a drawback, I saw as a plus. Our children at ages five and eight were far more independent than they ever would have been in the States. They could go on foot to visit friends, to nearby stores, and to school. I was glad we lived next door to the Morales family, who struggled with great dignity to cope with their limited economic possibilities. I was also grateful we lived near the jail and the orphanage, and that the children had the opportunity to be involved with me in starting the school. Largely as a result of spending those years in San Miguel de Allende, Kyria and Greta are both at home with all kinds of people from different cultures and nationalities.

4

I Move into Silence

Soon after school opened in San Miguel in the fall of 1973, Mother invited me to join her and two friends on a trip to visit the interior of New Guinea. While we were on a small riverboat, traveling down the Sepik River, she called me into the bathroom, where she was taking a shower. She had just noticed a lump in her right breast. I felt it too. She said that over fifty years before that moment, her own mother had asked Mother to feel her breast. Like me, Mother noticed her own mother's lump. Now I was thirty-six years old, and Mother was sixty-five. After the trip, Mother went to her clinic in New Orleans and immediately had a mastectomy. I felt horrible, but tried not to worry and hoped she would have no recurrence.

In early December of 1974, when we were just beginning to think about decorating for Christmas, Mother called to say her cancer had spread to her bones and liver. I knew she would die, but I didn't know how soon. Greta, at age six, saw I was devastated. As I put down the phone and burst into tears, she gave me her white woven "blanky" and told me to lie down on the little bench in our living room. "Go to sleep and don't even dream about Mamaw," she said. Kyria, who was then nine years old, was overwhelmed because she felt so close to her mamaw.

Mama and I in New Guinea, where she found a lump in her breast.

Me, meditating under the 'blessing tree'
by the pool, at home in Austin in 1987

During that same telephone conversation, Mother told me that through an organization called *Compassion*, she had found an eleven year old girl in Haiti exactly the same age as Kyria, whom she had just begun to support, hoping the Haitian child might become a pen pal with Kyria. In giving that gift, I think she was suggesting the importance of reaching out in personal ways to people in real need. We all knew that this would probably be her last gift to Kyria.

We immediately changed plans, closed our house in San Miguel, packed up the car and drove up to Houston to be with Mama. She looked so pale when we saw her at St. Luke's Hospital, hitched up to all sorts of tubes. One day, after visiting her in the hospital, Kyria looked up at that huge building as we were leaving and said, "There must be so many people in there who are sick, but out of all those people, for us, there is only one." Then, as we were driving back to Mother and Dad's house, she declared, "Mama, I want to become a cancer researcher so I can learn a way to prevent it." (Kyria now teaches Pilates, a special exercise program to help people strengthen their bodies.)

After Christmas my Dad, my husband, and the children went to Hickory Creek, our family place in Crockett, Texas, and left me alone with Mama. I was looking forward to having some good talks with her, but we were besieged with crises. One day, she fell three times. I hoped she would last at least until spring. I felt lost. I had always looked to Mother in times of distress, but this time she couldn't help me. Since we were no longer close to Horace Westwood, the Unitarian minister, and since I had no church affiliation, I knew of no one to guide us. It took courage for me simply to ask her at breakfast one morning, "Do you want to talk about what's happening?" She declined.

When I talked to Mother's friends Paul and Mildred Sherwood about how helpless I felt, they suggested Vipassana, clear inner seeing, a form of Buddhist meditation. Paul emphasized that learning to meditate took consistent practice. Whenever Mama went to sleep, I sat still on a cushion on the floor beside her trying to pay close attention to my breath, watching as it went in and out. I tried to let my thoughts pass through my head like birds, flying in one ear and out the other, as Paul suggested. I found a few moments of peace sitting on the floor near Mama as she was sleeping and dying.

When Dad, Hib, and the children came back from east Texas, just before New Year's, Mother had returned to the hospital. Hib then drove the children back to Mexico so they could be there in time for school. Until the end, I was always hopeful that something could be done to save Mama. The day after she moved back to the hospital, I saw my lawyer, Buck Arnold, in the elevator. When I told him how bad I felt that I had not taken her to M.D. Anderson, the cancer center in Houston, for a second opinion, he fussed at me. "Gretchen," he said, "do you think you are mightier than the rest of us? We all wish we could save your mother. But I'm not sure any of us can!" Just a few days later, on Epiphany, I awakened at five and hurried to St. Luke's Hospital in the cold and dark, without breakfast. I had a feeling Mama might die that day. I spoke to her for a few moments. Soon afterward, she slipped into a coma, then died on January 7, 1975.

The week following her death, the person I remember most vividly is Buck Arnold. He canceled his appointments and spent three days helping Dad and our whole family without ever counting the minutes. During that crisis, he became more than a lawyer to our family. He was like a brother to Dad and an uncle to me. Those days, I wasn't thinking of the body of Christ, but that's what his presence there with us means to me now. We weren't related, but he acted as if we were.

Once I got back to San Miguel, though I had hoped I would be able to let go of my feelings of loss I continued to feel devastated for months after Mama died. I missed her for Kyria's sake as well as mine. I remembered how my Dad's mother, Lucy Christine, after losing six of her children, told Dad, "Let's focus on the living." But I couldn't follow her example. If she could have, Mama would have whispered, "Forget about me and get on with your life." But I wasn't able to follow her imaginary command. I was aware that so often, hard as I tried, I could not even tune in when Kyria and Greta asked me a simple question. After a month of struggling, I spoke with one of Kyria and Greta's teachers, who suggested, "Just let yourself feel the pain totally. Write about your feelings. Stop condemning yourself for feeling guilty." Finally, after spending a few days writing about my unrealistic guilt, I began to get free.

This teacher's counsel was similar to one aspect of *Vipassana Buddhism*, which emphasizes watching our emotions instead of trying to control them. I learned this when I read an early draft of Paul Sherwood's book, *Falling Silent*. In it, he described his own experience with *Vipassana*. As a result of reading the draft and hearing about Paul and Mildred's experiences, I decided to attend a three-week silent meditation retreat in Litchfield, Connecticut. The Sherwoods' meditation master, Dhiravamsa, a Buddhist monk from Thailand, would lead it.

That spring, I left the children in San Miguel with Hib and Chucha, our maid, and joined thirty other people at the *Vipassana* retreat, which was held in a Catholic convent. We each had our own room with a tiny bed, a small window, a closet, and wash basin. In the beginning, we were told not to read or talk except during our daily visits with the meditation master. We would be sitting in meditation for over nine hours every day.

Our hour-long "sits" were interspersed with slow, mindful walks around the meditation hall and occasional lectures on Buddhism, given by Dhiravamsa. When I sat meditating, my breath was the focus. I was attentive to the cool air coming into my nostrils and the warmer air going out as I sat up

straight on my zafu (meditation pillow), with my legs crossed
on the floor.

I felt like a warrior learning her inner discipline. Dhiravamsa encouraged me to pay attention to each moment by
occasionally touching the center of my back, reminding me to
keep it straight. He sometimes whispered, "Relax and pay
attention." The first three days were like a battle against my
own thoughts, which kept interrupting the quiet. Dhiravamsa
explained that my work was not to fight the thoughts. My aim
then became to watch instead of resisting. When thoughts
took over, I tried to be compassionate toward myself by accept-
ing my noisy mind, especially my regrets. Finally, when I learned to let them be, they subsided, and my body relaxed. Learning
to value stillness has been one of my most important life lessons.
I have found comfort in the silence. Silence has been basic to
my prayer life and to my creative and philanthropic work as
well. Also, it has helped me not to feel lonely.

Quite opposite from my preconceptions, the purpose of
meditation was to help me face life's complexities, not to
remove me from them. Dhiravamsa taught us the same way
that he had been trained in Thailand. The first months of his
training had been spent in what he called "expressive meditation", which meant crying out pains from the past in order to
be more alive to the present. During my first retreat and future
ones, expressive work helped me to stop swallowing my pain
and to let go of my resentments against others and myself. The
very first time I was moved to go into the expression room
occurred when angry thoughts toward Mother's doctor came
up over and over. Finally, I left the quiet of the meditation hall
and went into the noisy expression room where the yelling and
crying of others stirred me to express my own feelings of
sadness and anger.

This expressive work has often helped me to get clear about
my life. Before Buddhist meditation, I used to hold in my

anger, following what I mistakenly believed was Gandhi's tradition of nonviolence. My work with Dhiravamsa helped me see, however, that I had been following neither the true Gandhi nor the true "me".

Those many hours I spent in Buddhist meditation readied me for the long silences that became part of my life during the days, weeks, and months I spent in a Catholic monastery after we moved back to the States in August of that same year (1975). I wanted to live in Houston near my dad. Also, the going back and forth every six months was disruptive.

Mother's death and our move to Austin, a city new to all of us, left me vulnerable and opened my heart to a new way. In 1976, when a new friend in Austin told me about the *Monastery of Christ in the Desert*, I was drawn to go there. Right away, I wrote to the guest master and arranged for a three-day visit. My friend had explained to me that it was a Benedictine monastery located in northern New Mexico, in a remote but beautiful spot between a river and steep cliffs. Only nine monks lived there, and there were usually no more than seven guests.

When I first arrived at the monastery in July 1977, two years after Mother died, I met the abbot, Brother Philip. He asked me about myself, and I told him I had recently become involved in Buddhist meditation and had just started going to an Episcopal Church in Austin. Immediately, he said I was welcome to bring my meditation pillow into the chapel, and sit on the floor. Brother Philip's openness surprised me and helped me make the transition from Buddhist meditation to Christian prayer. Prayer became for me like meditation with added touches of love. While praying, I sometimes felt a warmth, like a breeze that came, then passed. Having been invited to meditate in the chapel and to take communion with the brothers and other guests made me feel welcome from the beginning.

That first visit to the monastery was the beginning of many. Hib and I would leave Kyria and Greta at *Camp Cimarroncita* in New Mexico; then we would both head up to the monastery located just north of Taos. We used to stay at their guest house for anywhere between one and three weeks.

I felt at home sitting on the floor with some of the brothers who also had zafus. During the long pauses between the readings and prayers, I slipped naturally into meditation. The quiet, interspersed with prayers, reminded me of Quaker meetings my family went to when we lived in Pennsylvania. At Friends' meetings as well as at the monastery, I watched for signs of God's presence in the midst of quiet. Sometimes I noticed a feeling of tenderness, as if an invisible friend were beside me.

Of all the services, I especially remember Vigil. I loved joining the monks in prayer before dawn, then watching the change from dark to light through the chapel windows. Since I never set alarms, I depended on myself to wake up at 4 a.m. for the 4:30 service. When the chapel bell rang, fifteen minutes before the service began, I put on my clothes in a jiffy, grabbed my flashlight, then quickly walked from the guest-house to the chapel, a quarter of a mile away. The monks lit the kerosene lamps five minutes before the service began. As I was arriving, I would know the approximate time according to whether the windows of the chapel were glowing or dark. In the middle of Vigil, partly to keep awake, the monks played drums, marching around the chapel chanting, *"More than watch-men who wait for daybreak, we wait for you O Lord.* (Psalm 130:6)

This very early service lasted a little over an hour on weekday mornings, but longer on Sundays. The light of the kerosene lamps showed the monks in their loose sky blue shirts and lit their faces as they leaned over their booklets and chanted the words of the psalms.

After Vigil was Lauds, then Communion, followed by a breakfast of homemade bread, butter and café au lait. After breakfast, I often took a long walk that included a stop at a

*My room at
the monastery*

The guest house at the monastery

special place overlooking the Chama River. There, I read and pondered one of the Biblical passages I was carrying in my pocket. In the afternoon, I would look for another guest to join me in discussing the next day's readings. When the readings actually took place, we knew them almost by heart.

It was at the monastery that I first became familiar with Henri Nouwen's writings. One afternoon when I was cleaning the kerosene lanterns in the chapel, I happened to notice *Genesee Diary*, a book by Nouwen, lying beneath one of the benches. I looked through it and saw that Henri had committed himself to write a prayer each day when he went on a particular retreat. His commitment inspired me to write a prayer every morning after pondering the Bible readings. My prayers later became poems. For example, one day after breakfast, I found a spot of shade where I could sit outside beneath a tree to ponder Psalm 1:

Happy are those

who do not follow the advice of the wicked,

their delight is in the law of the Lord.

and on his law they meditate day and night.

They are like trees

planted by streams of water,

which yield their fruit in its season,

and their leaves do not wither.

In all that they do, they prosper. (Psalm 1:1-3)

I have always loved trees and imagined that tree trunks gave me strength. Because I compared them to my backbone, it was not much of a jump for me to move from the psalm to this prayer-poem:

Tree by the Waters

Yes Lord! the tree standing alone

by the flowing stream,

steady, upward reaching trunk.

Yes, I will stand firm,

my spine, its trunk.

Allow me to be deeply rooted,

and to reach down into cleansing

like the roots of the tree,

the one by the waters.

As I began to live more in the present, I became more like the tree by the waters. Then the words on Mother's tombstone gradually came true for me:

...unless a grain of wheat falls into the earth

and dies,

it remains just a single grain; but if it dies,

it bears much fruit.   (John, 12:24)

The feelings of loss I experienced after Mother's death stopped me in the midst of my busyness. The pain moved me to still- ness. In the midst of quiet, I learned to pray and began to write. It is still amazing for me to see how much good came from my most painful loss.

A smaller example of an ending that became a beginning occurred one evening as I was on my way to Compline, the last service of the day. I stopped in a field to look at a burst milkweed pod. Later that night as I was returning to the guesthouse, I looked up at the stars. It seemed pods had burst in the sky:

> Bursting Milkpods
>
> Milkpods burst!
>
> Cottons go straight
>
>> through the stars.
>>
>> There it is,
>>
>> that path swinging up and over
>>
>> from one horizon to the next.
>
> And I can feel them
>
>> sprinkling my hair
>>
>> as I dance back
>>
>> from Compline.

Remembering Compline makes me think of other endings, such as the death of Terese, my next-door neighbor in Austin. I became aware of Terese's difficulties just before Thanksgiving in 1978 when she called from an Austin hospital to say a doctor had operated and found a tumor the size of a grapefruit in her liver. Like Mother just a few years before, Terese had cancer. I was horrified and wanted to help her.

When she first got sick Terese asked me to pray for her. Before her operation and after, I took healthy food to her every day. But I wasn't sure how to pray for her. Didn't a prayer to save someone's life mean I had to be still for many hours and say exactly the right words? I also wondered if I had any right to bother God. Surely, God knew Terese was sick. Should I try to change God's mind if someone were dying? With Terese, as with Mama, I hoped with all my heart she would live, but I thought it would be haughty for me to tell God that. Brother

Michael, who had become my spiritual director at the monastery, explained that my constant hope that Terese would live, the tapes I made for her at the monastery, all the meals I had prepared, actually were prayers for her life. After that, I lost my shyness with God and joined the monks in prayers said aloud in the chapel. I called out my prayers for Terese, Kyria, Greta, my Dad, the monks, other guests, as well as for the people in El Salvador. (I had just become aware of the problems faced by people in Central America.)

The night Terese died, I was consoled in a beautiful way. Hib and I had just left the monastery. We invited Danny Regan, our Catholic priest friend, to join us for a short visit at the house we had rented in Santa Fe. Soon after we got there, Terese's husband called to say she had died. I had made a tiny altar in the corner of our living room with a piece of driftwood and a candle. Danny, although he had not known Terese, sat with me at my altar in silence for two hours, until eleven, that night.

Even before I went to the monastery, I had been concerned about my marriage. My husband was thoroughly disappointed that we had moved back to the States. He had become very moody because I was supporting the family financially. I sensed our marriage would not last. This possibility was frightening for me, and I was also afraid for the children, who were then ten and thirteen. Just as Brother Michael had encouraged me to pray for Terese, he made me feel it was also all right to pray for myself. After that, I began to look for ways to strengthen myself and to build my trust in God. Since my fear of being left alone had always been the largest obstacle for me in making changes in my life, it seemed to me that a good way for me to cope with my anxieties might be to experience complete aloneness. So I asked permission from the monks to stay across the Chama River, four miles from the monastery, in the rusty tiny trailer set up for their retreats.

I took rice, dried peas, onions, eggs, bread, fruit, and salt. To get there, I canoed across the Chama River, then walked down the canyon through the piñones to the trailer, which I called "the wee hut". It had been a house trailer. The main room had a little sink, a stove and a table that folded up and could be made into a bed. There was also a tiny room where there was a big Bible and a candle. I felt completely at ease during my three days there, both that first time in 1981, and then again for six days in 1982, partly because I knew the monks were praying for me every day.

Time passed quickly. I would get up before dawn, go outside and shiver as I looked up at the stars, then light the kerosene lamp in that tiny room with the big Bible. That's when I would write my prayer for the day. As it began to get light, I would go outside to sit and pray before breakfast. Feeling God's warmth during those prayer times was healing at a time when I still missed my mother and my marriage was in doubt. I was at home, sitting on that New Mexico ground. It was covered with piñon needles, and the brown needles evoked memories of sitting alone beneath other pine trees near my first home, on Memorial Drive in Houston. I began to see that many of the silent conversations that I had back then were really prayers, though I had never called them that.

The days across the river went by too fast. Before lunch, I would take another walk, fix my rice and split pea soup, then take a nap. Early in the afternoon, I would write more, in a shady spot down by a bend in the river. Late in the afternoon when it was hot, I went skinny-dipping in the Chama. After a light supper, I'd take another walk to see the sun drop and watch the stars fill the sky. Then I would read the Bible and write a prayer before sleep.

After a day in absolute quiet, noises in my head subsided. I felt happy to the point of bursting. I could not keep from singing, and I prayed not to lose my passion after leaving my retreat across the river:

Holy spirit, you have drawn me like wheat from the chaff.
Stay with me that I may be fruitful.

Being at the monastery and spending time across the river changed my life. Whereas before I had been hesitant even to enjoy a meal alone, afterwards I cherished solitude. Without that shift, I could not have begun to write or pray in earnest.

Returning to the monastery from across the river was like going home. Once again, I joined in the community, which had become my own. I always liked it when a single brother sang out in one of the services, *"Bear one another's burdens, for that is the law of Christ."* (Galatians 6:2). When I heard that chant, I sometimes remembered how Danny sat with me late into the night after Terese died. The chant mirrored our commitment to pray for one another, for the homeless, for people who were hungry, and for people living in violence. I liked the way the brothers called out their petitions spontaneously with a minute of quiet in between. This gave me time to find the heart of my concern so I also could call out my prayers. I felt more inspired to pray there than in my church at home, where prayers too often came from a book.

Many criticize such an intense focus on quiet prayer, saying that it tends to limit our involvement in the world. For me, the opposite is true. By being in the quiet of the monastery where others were praying for me, I learned to count on God's love, which steadied me so I could face personal challenges and reach out more effectively to others. When I got home, I began looking for people who, like me, wanted to pray together in silence, and who also wanted to translate Jesus's message into action. But first I had to face some hard realities in my own life.

The retreat place I called 'the wee hut'
at the Monastery of Christ in the desert

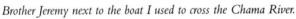

Brother Jeremy next to the boat I used to cross the Chama River.

5

The New Way

The jolt from Mama's death woke me up and moved me to silence. In the silence, I found more than comfort. I found the strength to act for myself, to take charge of my money, become closer to my Dad, and eventually to divorce my husband.

Right before Mama died, she told me how much she hoped we would get settled. Her thoughts coincided with my own wishes. I was happy we had had those years living in another country, but I saw that it would be good for the children to be in one school for several years and for me to be in one place so I could sink my teeth into something long-lasting. Changing countries and homes was not easy. The summer after Mother died, we sold our house in Mexico and returned to Texas to live in Austin.

At first we felt more like immigrants here than we had in Mexico. We had practically no friends in Austin besides my cousins, Standish and Sarah Meacham. Even after the children were enrolled in local public schools, we were still uneasy. We missed San Miguel, where we saw our friends every day without making arrangements. Chucha was no longer there to greet us with her delicious meals. And since we now lived several miles from town in a place where Greta and Kyria could no longer take off on foot, we became their chauffeurs.

We alternated between St. Michael's Episcopal Church and Quaker Meeting, but had no real church home. I was in the midst of learning to pray, and meditation was useful in helping me face the aloneness. My challenge was to "keep the faith" without a faith community.

Soon after we moved back to the States in 1976, I enrolled in the Graduate School of Social Work at the University of Texas. My hope was that a degree in social work would enable me to engage in community life in Austin in a more professional way than had been possible in Mexico and it did.

For example, in 1978, after I graduated, the *Austin Community School Program* employed me to organize a tri-ethnic festival in northeast Austin. I planned a big event designed to foster unity in a diverse community of Hispanics, Blacks and Anglos. Hundreds of children came with their parents. We had choirs, bands, piñatas, and ethnic dances.

Later the same year, *Meals on Wheels* hired me to organize their first two festivals. The idea behind these events was to raise money and public awareness about *Meals on Wheels*, which at that time served 290 homebound elderly citizens six meals every week. I was amazed that a small number of us could mobilize the whole city, from county commissioners to doctors, business people, journalists, radio and TV broadcasters. The second year, over six hundred people attended, and we made over $20,000. At the time, I didn't realize that we, all of us, were beginning a *Meals on Wheels* tradition that continues even today, more than twenty years later.

The job of planning those citywide festivals was enormous. It had taken me, working with over one hundred volunteers, almost three months to raise $20,000, and that was not even enough to pay the organization's director. It occurred to me then that perhaps there could be a reciprocal relationship between those who have money and those who desperately need it. Perhaps people with money would find meaning by giving their money away thoughtfully. I knew as well that community organizations that work with low-income people could do wonders with a monetary boost. For me, this was a "new way" of seeing the value of money. It showed me that it might be more helpful to give my money than my time.

As I began to see the great need for money in community service, I also began to feel some monetary pressure in my own life. Because of our more expensive life-style in the States and the fact that Hib had no salary, I was motivated to take a more active role in managing my money. Until then, I had left major decisions about finances in the hands of my Dad and the bankers. My husband had little interest in these matters. When I began more and more to take charge in the financial sphere, I was challenged and even frightened at times, because Dad had told me, over and over, that all of his sisters had been given a lot of money by his father and had lost it. Though there were no female models in my family to encourage me, it helped me to think back to my early years as a "businesswoman" on our small farm

Taking charge of my own money was far less challenging those days than dealing with my husband. He continued to be resentful that I was supporting our family. He disliked the commercial side of selling his paintings, and he decided once we had settled in Texas that he wanted to move to New Mexico where he might be inspired to paint. He did not want us to build a swimming pool, because he was worried about the image it would create. So when I began to think about building a pool to give Kyria and Greta a taste of the joy I had known as a child, I hesitated. I was afraid that having a pool might be wasteful, and more important, I didn't want to displease my husband.

I was frightened of change, scared of being lonely, and not sure I could manage on my own. During one of our separations, a voice kept saying, "Look how lonely you are. You better keep your job and your husband. You won't be able to manage alone." Some days, I felt so afraid that one minute took hours to pass.

Late one night, in the early eighties, my beloved friend and prayer partner, Judith Liro, appeared at my door in a thunderstorm. She led me back to my bedroom, where she lit candles, then suggested we both sit on the floor and pray together. She kept smiling, as if she knew a good secret. Then she gave me a passage from the gospel of Luke to read aloud:

> Now, he was teaching in one of the synagogues on the Sabbath. And just then, there appeared a woman with a spirit that had crippled her for eighteen years. She was bent over and was quite unable to stand up straight. When Jesus saw her, he called her over and said, "Woman you are set free from your ailment." When he laid his hands on her, immediately she stood up straight and began praising God.
>
> (Luke 13:10-13.)

As I read, Judith looked straight into my eyes and said, "Gretchen, you also are set free. Like peasants in Central America, you have bent over backwards to please your husband for too long. Stand up straight. From this moment, your life will be different." Judith's timing and choice of reading was uncanny. I was amazed. I felt freed!

Energy to make changes in my life was boosted by the assertive spirit I had learned in Vipassana meditation and by the strength I had found in studying the Bible, praying with the monks and being alone in the quiet of the monastery.

Even so, I hesitated to act assertively until Judith and other friends pointed out that Kyria and Greta would most likely use me as their role model. It had taken me a long time to realize that inaction does not always lead to peacefulness. If it did, it would mean that women in difficult marriages should *shut-up*

My beloved friend, Judith Liro

and oppressed people should quietly accept their plight. Would I want to suggest to my daughters, even indirectly, that they should cover up the unacceptable in their own lives?

A few months before I made my final decision to divorce Hib, I went to see my Dad at Hickory Creek. While I was there, Hib called me, angrily attempting to persuade me to continue in our marriage. The day after his call, I visited Mother's grave. As I worked at resetting the bricks bordering her gravesite, I composed a poem:

Setting Boundaries

I felt deeply alone without her

and feared the loss of him.

His words, like that hot August sun,

kept pounding

as I labored

pulling out bricks,

resetting them firmly in line

clearly establishing the boundary

around Mother's grave.

As I set those bricks,

his harsh words from the night before

threatened my own blurred boundaries.

Taught by pain, livened by work,

I turned to tending my boundaries.

As I wrote this poem, I decided to tell Dad I was separated from Hib and that our separation might end in divorce. I was afraid he would disapprove. Instead, he was completely supportive. Still, I wavered. I worried that if I divorced Hib I would feel the loss for a long time afterward.

I took a cue from Dad's self-confident way of managing his money and his life. I was impressed when I saw him taking charge of his monthly board meetings in Houston. It was a different world and I enjoyed it. I admired the way Dad orchestrated discussions by balancing executive decisiveness with a collaborative style. He encouraged questions and made sure we all got clear answers. At lunch after the meeting, I usually had friendly and informative conversations with men from TESCO, my father's company, as well as with Dad's lawyer, Buck Arnold, and banker, J.W. Link.

In the midst of business, Dad was never too preoccupied to remember personal touches. At a special moment after lunch, he would whisper to Turner, the waiter, to bring a bag of macaroons "to go." When Turner delivered the small brown bag to me, Dad would announce, "Be sure Kyria and Greta get these cookies. Tell them they're from Grandaddy, and tell'em," he would say with tears in his eyes, "I sure do love 'em both!"

Greta playing with her grand-dad

It was the example of my dad, a superb businessman and a loving man, that convinced me that money and love don't have to be rivals. As I began to realize this, I remembered the moment after my college graduation when Aunt Ethel spoke to me about how important it was, both for me and for Mother, that I thank her for the diamond ring instead of rejecting her gift and my heritage. Finally, twenty-one years later, I was ready to absorb Aunt Ethel's loving suggestion. I realized I did not have to choose either/or. I could be grateful for my heritage, symbolized by that tiny diamond ring, while also standing up for distant neighbors.

My old tendency to disparage money had been partly prompted by seeing thousands of people in developing countries barely existing without medical care, adequate food or housing. This had made me feel guilty about having money myself, so guilty, in fact that I tried to ignore it all together. Then it occurred to me that as long as I had money and others were dying for the lack of it, it was wrong for me not to pay close attention to it. Finally, as I began to see that money could even be an instrument of love, I found it easier to carry out what I felt God was calling me to do. By investing wisely, I saved enough money to start *Expanding Horizons,* a small philanthropic foundation, in 1983. When I began to use my money for outreach, I felt freer to spend it for my own family too. That's when I realized outreach and personal enjoyment could be compatible.

As I began to see money in this new way, I thought about my Grandfather Shartle, who playfully referred to money as *filthy lucre.* He was the first person in our family to make a lot of money. By reading his unpublished stories, I have learned how he and my grandmother, Lucy Christine, responded to people who came to their back door asking for help. They always gave them a plate of food. I am tempted to wonder if besides giving them food he might have given these men a skill by using his machine company as a training site for an apprenticeship program. Nevertheless, I remain grateful for his generosity to my father who in turn was generous to me.

For me, the first step in finding my way was to become a Christian. That commitment helped me find the strength necessary to make big changes like moving back to the states and beginning a creative life in Austin. I saw a new dimension in the value of money, all the while growing in closeness with God. My quiet and my active lives came together. That was the period when I became actively involved with Central America. Without my knowing it then, this new way became the foundation for the rest of my life.

6

My American Dream is Shattered

Just when I was beginning to settle into *the new way*, Kyria, without meaning to, started me on a venture that further changed my life. While studying at a Washington D.C. boarding school, she was chosen to represent Nicaragua at a mini-United Nations conference in Washington. She asked me to help her. Since I had hardly heard of Nicaragua, I went to the Austin Central Library to research the subject. What I learned then, and confirmed in subsequent years, was a blow to my American dream.

My faith in America and my faith in God were intertwined. Since childhood, I had seen the United States as the place where oppressed people found freedom and justice, truly a "promised land." We were the nation that had come up with the Marshall Plan to help our World War II enemies get back on their feet. In the *Declaration of Independence*, the *Constitution,* and the *Bill of Rights*, our forebears gave us the foundations for the most vibrant democracy the world had ever seen. Many nations around the world have drawn inspiration from our example. Practically everywhere I had gone in my travels, people had liked me more when they learned I was an American.

That day at the library, I was shocked to learn how shameful our role in Nicaragua had been. I found, for instance, that my

Kyria at school, 1980

government had almost always sided with Nicaragua's dictatorial regimes, interfering in that country's internal affairs for over seventy years. From 1909-1912 the U.S. government had engineered the replacement of two elected presidents. It had also ignored the ruling of the Central American Court that condemned the placement of U.S. Marines in Nicaragua in 1912. And there was more. In 1933, the United States government set up the Nicaraguan National Guard under the command of Anastasio Somoza. That marked the beginning of forty-six years of U.S. support for the dictatorship of the Somoza family.

The U.S. continued to back the National Guard and the Somoza family dynasty in Nicaragua even after it became well-known that they were responsible for unbelievable atrocities. Anastasio Somoza had shown his ruthlessness before he became the dictator of Nicaragua in the mid-1930's. He engineered the killing of Augusto César Sandino, Nicaragua's most revered hero, famous for leading groups that were opposed to U.S. intervention. (The "Sandinista" movement took its name from Sandino ... to keep alive his nationalist struggle.)

When the U.S. Marines left in 1933, Sandino signaled his readiness to negotiate with Somoza. Trusting that his safety would be guaranteed, he came down from hiding in the mountains to work out a peace agreement. To make sure it would come about, Anthony Bliss Lane, the U.S. Ambassador to Nicaragua, exacted from Somoza his pledge that Sandino would not be harmed. That same day, Anastasio Somoza ordered the officers of the National Guard to kill Sandino. They yanked him from his car, along with two of his generals, took them to a nearby field, and shot them. Somoza claimed he had received approval from Lane.

As if that weren't enough, the National Guard massacred Sandino's troops and many of their families, who were establishing agricultural cooperatives in a northern rural area. In spite of Anastasio Somoza's violence and cruelty, the United States government continued to support him. Even after his son, Anastasio Somoza Debayle ("Tachito") and his followers embezzled millions of dollars from United States aid money, which had been earmarked for the reconstruction of Managua following the dreadful earthquake of 1972, the backing of the United States was never in question.

Meanwhile, large segments of the Nicaraguan people began to express their revulsion for the Somozas. "Tachito's" corruption and a shift in the Catholic Church played major roles in their awakening. After the Second Vatican Council (1962-65), the church began to follow the Bible more closely and to support the rights of the poor. Grass roots Christian groups called *base ecclesial communities* found biblical inspiration for the building of a just society. Nicaraguan Christians finally came to understand that Somoza's dictatorship was an offense to God and humanity.

Christians became a large part of a broad leadership called the *Frente Sandinista de Liberación Nacional* (the *FSLN*). This was the revolutionary force which since the early sixties had taken up the unfinished struggle of coalition-building for which even Somoza and the National Guard were no match.

In the summer of 1979, many Americans were jolted into awareness. The event that catalyzed U.S. public opinion was the killing of Bill Stewart, the ABC-TV correspondent in Managua, on June 20, 1979. Forty-five years after Somoza had engineered the murder of Sandino, Stewart was pulled out of his car, made to kneel, then shot through the head by members of the National Guard who had seen him filming compromising scenes. What the guardsmen did not know was that Stewart's camera crew filmed the killing, then aired it on world-wide TV. This display of utter contempt for human life could not be erased from the hearts and minds of millions of Americans. Even then, the U.S. was one of the last countries to withdraw its support for the Somoza family.

Once our government wavered in its support of the Somoza dynasty, the Nicaraguan opposition began to succeed in their efforts to overthrow him. The nation celebrated victory on July 19, 1979. During the course of the conflict, over forty thousand Nicaraguans were killed, out of a population of around 3.5 million people. This would be the equivalent of over four million deaths in the United States. Around a hundred thousand Nicaraguans were wounded and one fifth of the population became homeless. The Somozas, together with the National Guard, had almost destroyed the economy and left the new government with a debt to the United States of 1.5 billion dollars, which the new Nicaraguan government proceeded to pay back in record time. The victors took the high road. They executed no one, handed out relatively short sentences, and permitted no acts of vengeance, even against the National Guard officers.

Then, something ominous occurred even as Nicaraguans were still celebrating their new day. Most of Somoza's National Guard fled immediately to Honduras, across the northern border of Nicaragua. Soon after, in 1981, the Reagan administration began to organize them as counter-revolutionaries, hence the name "contras" by which they came to be known.

By 1982, I was seeing parallels between Nicaragua of the 20th century and United States of the 18th century. Both countries played David-like roles against their respective Goliaths. In the 18th century, England was the oppressor of the United States; in the 20th century, the United States was the oppressor of Nicaragua. Even with history to teach us better, two-hundred plus years after the United States had won independence, it was denying to the Nicaraguans the right to their hard-won freedom.

As I learned these things, my patriotism began to waver. I sent Kyria the results of my research. She knew nothing of the

horrors of World War II, but I did. Inspired by our victory over
regimes that brutalized those who had no power, I had decided
as far back as the late forties that if ever my country played the
role of aggressor without justification, or treated any group of
people unjustly, I would speak out. Perhaps it was because of
our difference in ages or the difference in our historical con-
texts that while this material hardly fazed Kyria, it changed my
life. I had to get involved. What was happening was clearly
unjust and cruel. I thought back to the Monastery of Christ,
where I learned that prayer, faith and justice are inseparable.
Remembering this gave me a fresh sense of direction. As I
began to move forward, a helpful pattern evolved. It was first to
learn, then to pray, finally to act.

My friend, Randy Taylor, aptly described this point in my
life when he said, "You were trying to be a good mom, and
then to your surprise, you became an activist." True, but before
taking action, I knew I had to learn more. In order to do just
that, I started a bi-weekly lunch group with Barbara Aldave,
our neighbor and a professor at the University of Texas School
of Law. The focus of our gatherings was recent developments
in Nicaragua and El Salvador. We constantly asked ourselves
one question: what can we do to make more people aware of
this situation?

We invited several speakers, including an Episcopal priest
from North Carolina named Henry Atkins. As I was introduc-
ing him in the LBJ School auditorium, I remembered how the
prophet Jeremiah had called out to his hard-headed people,
"Circumcise yourselves to the Lord, remove the foreskin of your
hearts." (Jeremiah 4:4). To my amazement, I heard myself yelling
to the audience, "Circumcise yourselves!" I wanted people to
open their hearts to the hideous suffering our government was
inflicting on the Central American people. (My friend Judith
Liro still reminds me, "You sure got our attention!")

I kept reading everything I could find on Central America.

That's how I learned that, beginning in 1981 President Reagan had started a campaign to convince the world that the U.S.S.R. was sending weapons to Salvadoran opposition groups via Cuba and Nicaragua. Key U.S. national security officials did not hesitate to create evidence to justify a dubious policy. President Reagan himself worked with the U.S. State Department to publish a "white paper" report called *Communist Interference in El Salvador*. It was released February 23, 1981. Reagan never swayed from it, even though a newspaper as conservative as the *Wall Street Journal* called it "a tarnished report" (Jonathan Kwitny, *Wall Street Journal*, June 8, 1981). Other major newspapers also called attention to its flaws. The *Nation* put it this way:

> The white paper is a thin tissue of falsifications, distortions, omissions and simplifications directed toward covering up increased U.S. support for a murderous regime. It has sought to transform a war between the regime and its people into an East-West struggle and to deny the internal socio-economic and political roots of the struggle. The purpose of these distortions is to mobilize U.S. public opinion behind the new administration's policies not only in El Salvador but throughout the third world.
>
> (The *Nation*, March 28,1981, p. 335)

David C. MacMichael, a CIA analyst during the years 1981-83, lost his job because he refused to create evidence to show that arms were being shipped from Nicaragua into El Salvador. He refused to lie. Since he could not comply with superior orders, he left the CIA. On June 11, 1984, he was quoted in the *New York Times* as follows:

> There has not been a successful interdiction, or a verified report of arms moving from Nicaragua to El Salvador since April 1981. The Administration and the CIA have system- atically misrepresented Nicaraguan involvement in the supply of arms to Salvadoran guerrillas to justify efforts to overthrow the Nicaraguan Government.

To stop this alleged flow of arms, Reagan authorized U.S. training of the contras. Mike Conroy, then a professor at the *University of Texas Institute of Latin American Studies*, told me that in February 1981 the Reagan administration had begun funding over seven thousand Contras then living in Honduran refugee camps just north of the Nicaraguan border. Their average pay was $600 per month, roughly ten times what local Honduran workers earned. Later, in 1982, the Reagan administration authorized support for the Contras in excess of $5 million. In 1983, again at Reagan's request, Congress provided $24 million and in 1986, $100 million, for the Contras.

I wondered if Mike was idealizing the Sandinista government, especially when he said that Nicaraguan student volunteers had gone by the hundreds to rural areas where they were teaching thousands of people to read and write. He also told me there were numerous painters and poets of international renown in Nicaragua, including Ernesto Cardenal, the Minister of Culture, whom I would later meet. I had heard and read so many negative descriptions of the new Nicaraguan government that it was hard for me to believe such positive accounts could be true.

By 1983, I knew I should go to Central America. Otherwise I would always be wondering if what I read or what I heard was actually true. Still, I was hesitant. I was in the middle of a divorce and going meant leaving Greta, who was then fifteen. She was scared I might get killed. Kyria was away at school so she was not as involved. Mike had told me there were Contra attacks and some killings on the Honduran border, particularly near Jalapa. I was genuinely concerned, but I knew my commitment to Central America would remain in limbo until I went to see for myself. I decided to join a trip recommended by Henry Atkins and planned by the *Carolina Inter-Faith Task Force on Central America*. To be honest, I was apprehensive about traveling with a group of complete strangers to a country being attacked by my own government.

100

*Internationally renowned poet, Ernesto Cardenal,
and Minister of Culture to Nicaragua*

Greta, at age 15, when I left for Nicaragua

My first evening in Managua, in March 1983, a Nicaraguan woman approached me on the street and pleaded with me to tell Mr. Reagan to stop sending down the guns and ammunition, because they were being used to kill her people. That night, I remembered the day I arrived in Paris, on July 14th (*Bastille Day*) in 1955. The French people were genuinely happy to meet me, because I was an American and from Texas to boot. I was even praised for my country's major role in liberating the French ten years before. What a contrast!

Because I had promised Greta I would not go to the Honduran border, where the Contras were staging attacks into Nicaragua, I stayed by myself in Managua while others in our group went to Jalapa. The morning they left, I sat on the floor of the small room that I shared with eighteen other women. There, I lit a fat pink candle and placed it on the lower bunk of my bed. That became my altar where I prayed for our group, and for Greta, Kyria, myself, and the Nicaraguan people.

While our group was at the border, I visited some *base ecclesial communities* in Ciudad Sandino, an unincorporated community just outside Managua. That Sunday night, seven meetings took place simultaneously in the parish. Each group of about twenty people began by singing hymns led by a guitarist. Then the gospel lesson designated for that day was read. It was about Jesus' call to forgive our enemies. People discussed their fear of the Contras and grieved over the many killings they had committed, then prayed for them. I thought, "It's hard enough for me to pray for someone who has hurt me emotionally. It would be impossible for me to pray for people who were killing my friends, my children, and also destroying everything I had worked to build."

The North Carolina group returned from the border horrified by the devastation caused by the Contras. Right away, we started to plan a non-violent strategy that would help the Nicaraguans and also get the attention of the American people.

Our chance came immediately. We met with Tomás Borge, the Minister of Internal Affairs. That's when a member of our group suggested Americans could form a constant international presence along the border between Nicaragua and Honduras. The idea was to report Contra raids first-hand and share the risk of being killed by U.S. bullets. Borge immediately replied, "No, we do not want any of you to be killed." I believe that if the Contras had killed an American in Nicaragua, the publicity would have helped the Sandinistas galvanize American public opinion against the Contras. The negative publicity might even have forced the United States to cut its support to the Contras.

We met with a broad spectrum of organizations and leaders including the American ambassador and a diversity of newspaper editors and political parties, some supportive and some critical of the Sandinistas. We heard Sandinista leaders explain that their country was organizing according to "the logic of the majority," while the Somoza dictators had ruled according to the logic of the elite.

The "logic of the majority" meant making striking reforms in literacy and health. Before the revolution, Nicaragua had the highest rate of infant mortality in Central America. Through its health programs, the Sandinista government cut infant mortality by one third and had miraculous successes with their literacy crusade. Within one year after the revolution, 100,000 student volunteers went to rural areas where they lived for six months, often in primitive conditions, as they taught reading and writing to whole communities. The effectiveness of their work showed. At the start of the campaign, only thirty-five percent of the people were literate. Within one year, the new government had increased the literacy rate to eighty-eight percent. (Figures from the *1986 Annual Report of the Inter-American Development Bank*.)

Before I left for Nicaragua, Dr. William Glade, the director of the *Institute of Latin American Studies at the University of Texas*, gave me a letter of introduction to Dr. Valentín Lara who was a

pediatrician in León. I was happy when I learned our group
would be visiting León, because that gave me a chance to meet
the Laras. Right away, I was impressed by their youngest daughter,
Magali who, at age nine, was the youngest student volunteer in
the nation to participate in the literacy crusade. I admired her
for having the gumption to live with strangers in primitive
conditions, far away from her family, in order to teach poor
people. I also respected her parents for allowing her to go.

For so many years the majority of Nicaraguans had mourned
the deaths of their babies, tilled the land for others, and lived
without freedoms we take for granted. Finally, they had hope,
because they had tasted the fruits of a "promised land." Nevertheless, they were still struggling against the U.S. government
and its support of the Contras in Honduras.

We all felt drawn to help. Our last night in Nicaragua, the
leader of our group, Gail Phares, who was a staunchly dedicated
Catholic fighter for human rights, encouraged us to write our
representatives. She suggested that we tell them what we had
learned and also that we make appointments to see them. She
had even brought typewriters for that purpose! We all worked
until way after midnight, then helped each other edit the
letters. I wrote to our Texas Senator, Lloyd Bentsen, who was
then on the U.S. Senate Intelligence Committee, and to his
chief legislative aid. I also wrote Buck Arnold, who was a close
friend of Bentsen's. In addition, I sent reports to congressional
offices all over the U.S. That last night, we also began to plan
our next trip to Nicaragua, which would take place on the fourth
of July that same year, 1983. I hoped to go on that trip, too.
Once I got home, I missed Gail Phares and the Carolina group.
I felt lonely in Austin, where few people shared my new fervor.
I was glad to see Greta, of course, and she was relieved to see
me all in one piece. But I wasn't completely sure how she felt
until she told me in a telephone conversation from camp that
summer, "Mama, I feel so proud of you when I talk to other

campers here and tell them about your work with Central America. None of their moms are doing anything like that." That conversation eased my anxiety, but I knew my new version of patriotism would still make it hard for me to be seen as a "normal mom."

After this first trip, the most frustrating thing for me was the indifference of so many Americans. When I spoke to a friend at church about the issues involved and encouraged her to think about them when she voted, she wrote me a letter in which she said, "These issues do not affect me, so why should I vote with them in mind?" People in my church prayed for their own friends and families, but practically no one prayed for distant neighbors like the people in Central America. "Why settle for either/or?" I wondered.

One reason people seemed to care so little for the plight of Central Americans may have been inadequate news coverage. News of the alleged Communist threat dominated most reports about Central America. Atrocities caused by the military in El Salvador and by the Contras in Nicaragua were given little or no visibility. Also, the accomplishments in the new Nicaragua were hardly reported in the United States. Those days, although I watched television, listened to National Public Radio, and read three newspapers daily, I saw no reports about the Literacy Crusade or the Sandinista health programs. There were times when I thought that what we had seen in Nicaragua must have been an illusion, since it was diametrically opposite to the reports we kept hearing in the U.S. However, these doubts vanished as I got more involved. The necessity to move forward became clear.

7

I Should Have Been Afraid

When I became convinced that our government's stance in Central America was irrational and destructive, I decided not to sit still, as I had during the Vietnam War. I looked for ways to make our voices heard. I decided that the best way was to invite Americans in leadership positions to visit Central America. After seeing with their own eyes what was really happening, I believed they would realize how misguided the U.S. government was, and they would tell others what they had seen. I was confident this strategy would eventually help to change our policy.

The pattern was clear. In both Nicaragua and El Salvador, the United States was supporting the oppressors. In Nicaragua ... it backed members of Somoza's National Guard ... known as the Contras. In El Salvador, it chose to support the existing government, even though it had come to power by largely unlawful means. In both cases, the justification was an alleged communist threat. In pursuit of that objective, the U.S. government and its regional allies in Central America did not hesitate to violate internationally recognized legal norms.

The reports I heard from El Salvador in the early eighties were more horrifying than the news we were getting from Nicaragua. From church groups, I had received many photographs of Salvadoran bodies - bodies allegedly dismembered by the Salvadoran military. Salvadoran military forces committed the atrocities and the United States paid the bills. I stored reports of those atrocities in my office closet. One night, I heard agonizing screams in my dream coming from my closet. The long arm of legalized terrorism had reached into my home.

People hesitated to believe me when I told them some of the reports I had heard, so it may be helpful to include other reports documented by the American Friends Service Committee:

> Nine hundred seventy-five Salvadoran soldiers and officers received three months of training from January through March, 1981, at Fort Bragg, North Carolina and Fort Benning, Georgia. This training cost the U.S. tax payers fourteen million dollars. The soldiers were armed with M-16 rifles, M-60 machine guns, M-79 grenade launchers, and 90 mm. automatic machine guns. When they returned to El Salvador, they were sent to the northern part of Chaletenango where they then killed 600 unarmed refugees. (*The Central American War: A Guide to the U.S. Military Buildup."* AFSC, p. 6)

Another report in the same document describes a press conference organized by the Salvadoran Human Rights' Commission in September 1982, at which women told about a massacre in August 1982, where 300 women and children were killed. A refugee woman spoke:

> When we were trying to run, we could not get by the soldiers. They fired on us and threw grenades at us from all directions. We kept trying to escape with our children. Just when we were getting out, a helicopter passed over us. When we were going down the hill, soldiers blocked us off and surrounded us. It was an ambush. We were there for a long time. We saw death, and death saw us. When people tried to run away through the valleys, soldiers corralled them. They killed a real mountain of people: children, old men and women. Many people jumped over the cliff trying

to save themselves. At night, they bombarded people using lights so they could see, and wherever they saw people hiding, they shot them.

(*The Central America War, A Guide to The U.S. Military Buildup.* AFSC. p. 3)

A report I heard on National Public Radio in 1982 brought home the violence in Central America with awful clarity. A woman who lived outside San Salvador had been killed, then cut into pieces. Her body had been thrown onto a garbage dump, then eaten by dogs. As I listened, I remembered María, who had helped us when we lived in Mexico. Her body had been tossed onto a garbage dump. I was determined that no more Marías would suffer. I had read enough about El Salvador to know that this story was not an isolated horror, but was an example of what was happening to thousands of people.

The epistle reading at my church the day I heard that report happened to be Corinthians 6:19, "Do you not know that your body is a temple of the Holy Spirit within you, which you have from God?" I realized that I felt related to that unnamed woman thrown onto the garbage dump way down in El Salvador, and I was disappointed that people in my church didn't want to hear her story.

My pastor, who had heard me refer to victims of the Central American conflict over and over during the prayers of the people, called me into his office and asked why I was concerned about events so far away. He asked if I had a problem in my personal life and intimated that I was displacing my attention from my personal anxieties to a distant problem. I told him that regardless of any problems I might have in my own life, I was still very angry at my government for supporting so much destruction in Central America. I never stopped talking, as he hinted I should. It was so hard to talk about these things that when I did I sometimes stuttered. Later, I wrote a poem:

Where is the Real Temple?

Is only Jesus' body the temple,
his heart the altar?
What about that dark woman,
the ugly one just killed,
is God in her too?

Are only Jesus' ribs the temple?
What about the murdered Salvadoran woman?
Is it all right to speak out for her?
Taboo - shh -
Pray and pray, then speak secretly of her.

Soldiers cut her, gutted her,
threw her to dogs.
Was her body holy too?

How can we find God?
only through ritual, preaching and creeds?

Where is the real temple?

The more I came to believe that every person's body is a temple
of the Holy Spirit, the more determined I became to spread
the truth about what was happening in Central America.

I did not realize then that soon I would meet a man far more
passionate and able in standing up for people in Central America than I was. I first heard about this man from my friend
Frank Sugeno, a professor at the Episcopal seminary in Austin.

Frank had told me about his friend Jorge Lara-Braud a few months before I went to Nicaragua in 1983. Jorge then lived in Atlanta, where he was serving as the director of the *Council on Theology and Culture of the Presbyterian Church of the United States*. Frank suggested I write and invite Jorge to dinner during one of his trips to Austin. Frank told me that Jorge had been sent several times as an emissary to El Salvador for the *World and National Councils of Churches*. This had enabled him to meet and then later to become a close friend of Archbishop Romero of El Salvador. Frank explained that Romero had received many death threats after he announced to the army that they should obey God rather than their military leaders, who were ordering them to kill. Frank said Jorge had pleaded with Romero in late 1979 to come to the States for safety, but he had declined. As long as his flock remained without security, he could not seek it for himself. Romero was shot in the heart and head by a sniper on March 24,1980, while officiating at a Memorial Mass for the mother of a friend.

I had written to Jorge as Frank suggested, but I never expected to hear from him. He said to me later that when he saw my letter, he told his secretary to tell this lady in Austin that he would be too busy to see her when he was there. However, he called the day after I returned from my first trip to Nicaragua. We met for about an hour before he began his presentations as the 1983 Heinsohn Lecturer at the *University Methodist Church* in Austin. His lectures focused on the role of the church in the Central American conflict. Right away I was smitten and hoped he was too, although I imagined I was probably far too ordinary for the likes of him. The next day, Greta and I heard his sermon, which was based on Matthew 6:27: "Consider the lilies of the field, how they grow; they neither toil nor spin." It touched my heart to find a man of tenderness also concerned about such big issues as the war in El Salvador. Later I realized that, for him, the two went together.

He called Greta and me into the minister's office between services so we could get to know each other. That's when he told us a story of four teenage boys and their priest who were killed by the Salvadoran military while at a Catholic retreat. Afterwards, the government covered up this "dirty work" by publishing a story stating that these boys were really guerilla fighters. This particular story, about the killing of children roughly the ages of my Kyria and Greta, persuaded me even more that it was urgent to get out the facts.

During his lectures, Jorge told many stories to build a historical context. He explained that the Salvadoran people had been living in a state of conflict with wealthy landowners since the Spanish conquest. During the one hundred year period from 1870 to 1970, the largest landowners succeeded in forcing the small farmers off their properties so the landowners could produce more coffee, cotton, and sugar for export. By 1971, sixty-four percent of the land belonged to four percent of El Salvador's landowners. By the end of the 1970's, sixty percent of the people who had traditionally depended on land for their livelihood had none, or less than a subsistence plot.

Jorge explained that the people of El Salvador had time and again used nonviolent means to press their demands for land reform, a living wage, democracy, and education. When peasants in the western part of the country held a demonstration in 1932, the military responded by killing over thirty thousand of them in what Salvadorans still call *la matanza* (the massacre).

In a large part of Latin America, people despaired until they began to hear the hopeful notes of the Second Vatican Council (1962-1965). Before Vatican II, poor people believed it was their mandated duty to accept their plight. The Catholic laity were not permitted to read or discuss scripture, but depended on priests to understand their faith for them. Then, after Vatican II, the church shifted from an alignment with the wealthy few and the military to a defense of the poor. As in Nicaragua,

Archbishop Romero with children

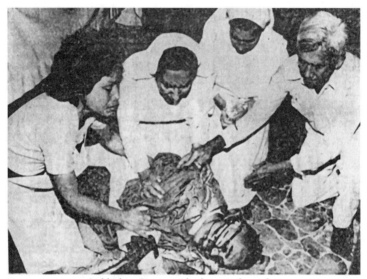

Archbishop Romero who has just been shot

ordinary Christians formed *base ecclesial communities*, where they learned that the prophets and Jesus wanted all people to have fruitful lives.

This church shift encouraged Salvadoran peasant leagues, student groups, and labor unions to organize and demand basic reforms. Twice in the 1970's, coalitions of popular groups won presidential elections; twice the military took away their victories. In spite of such setbacks, representatives of the people kept on trying to meet with government representatives. Jorge described one of those meetings:

> On November 27 in 1980, when we were celebrating Thanksgiving in the United States, representatives of Salvadoran popular groups risked negotiating with the army and government officials. The place chosen was a Jesuit high school in downtown San Salvador. These representatives got to the meeting first. While they were waiting, over two hundred soldiers arrived and killed them all. At that point, many of their friends, inspired by their sacrifice and by the Christian message of social justice, moved into the hills and took up arms against the military government. That was in 1980 and 1981.

Jorge brought this event home to us by using an illustration from our own history:

> It was as though the British had said to the Continental Congress: "Come let us reason together in Philadelphia," only to turn that into an ambush where no American patriot came out alive. The United States did nothing to put pressure on the Salvadoran government to bring the killers to account. In this way, we gave the signal it was O.K. to kill as long as they placed a communist label on the victims. Pressured by Congress, the Carter Administration resumed military aid to the Salvadoran government, and by 1983 the Reagan administration was sending El Salvador around one million dollars a day in war-related assistance.

On March 25, 1980, the day after Archbishop Romero was

assassinated, Jorge testified to a subcommittee of the House of Representatives. He reemphasized what the Archbishop had said in his letter to President Carter imploring him not to allow more money to be sent for the military buildup in El Salvador. However, the subcommittee voted for resumption of aid.

After these lectures, Jorge and I began to write letters and make phone calls to each other. Finally, he was able to stop by Austin on his way to another destination. During that first visit, Greta stayed home from school because she had a cold. This meant she could spend several hours listening to Jorge tell about Archbishop Romero's funeral at the cathedral in San Salvador. He described how the military began to fire just above people's heads, into the crowded square facing the cathedral. So many people crowded into the cathedral that there was little breathing room. Smaller people, mostly women, jammed between the bodies of larger people, began suffocating.

Jorge felt someone behind him tugging on the sleeve of his robe. He turned around to see a woman suffocating. She believed he was a priest. He knew she wanted last rites, so he made the sign of the cross and whispered words of forgiveness. She died instantly. He and others lifted the woman's body up over people's heads to a place outside of the cathedral. There, she was put on a pile with the many others who had died the same way. When the shooting died down, Jorge and Bishop Samuel Ruiz from Chiapas, Mexico, walked out of the cathedral arm in arm. Jorge was shattered when he saw a small boy hugging the dead body of his mother. Jorge wept, and Bishop Ruiz, who was watching, yelled, "Those murderers have crucified Him again, but He will rise again!"

Soon after I met Jorge, the Carolina Interfaith Task Force organized their second trip to Nicaragua. On this second trip, they aimed to include people from all over the United States. I was amazed when Jorge agreed to join us, because he was busy with his job at the Presbyterian Church headquarters in Atlanta.

Aftermath of the attack, inside the cathedral

*The Cathedral Plaza, nearly deserted after
the attack on the day of Romero's funeral*

I remember seeing him when he first appeared with the group from Georgia. They were all wearing tee shirts that said, *"No one is safe until we are all safe!"* We had gone with 150 people from all over the United States.

The purpose of this second trip was not only to stand in solidarity with the Nicaraguan people, but also to let more people from our country see Nicaragua's struggle firsthand. Our goal was audacious. We wanted to stop the violence of the Contras at its source, at least for a day, and hopefully longer. We would travel to the Honduran border to make a human chain with local people, thus symbolically protecting the Nicaraguans. That could be the most effective way to let Americans learn what was at stake.

During this second trip, once again I really was not afraid of being killed, but if I should be, I did not want my death to be useless. Half seriously, I asked my closest friends to put my body on Reagan's desk if something unforeseen should happen to me! Deep down, I was scared, more for Kyria and Greta than for me. When it dawned on me that I really might be killed, I realized the only person I trusted enough to care for my children was my Dad, but he was old, it would be hard. These realities made me feel self-protective. I was almost as apprehensive as I had been during the first trip when I considered going to Jalapa where the war was going on. To prevent us from being killed by one of our own bullets, Jorge spent many hours meeting with government officials before the trip, arranging for our protection.

I was concerned about the trip to the border, but finally decided I did not want to stay back in Managua, as I had on the first trip, while my group went to Jalapa. My worries about security faded after a pleasant surprise. Henri Nouwen had come to hear Jorge speak in a Managua Baptist church and he went up to say hello afterwards. While I was waiting for Jorge I saw him pulling Henri by the hand up into the bus. Jorge knew

I had read many of Nouwen's books when I was at the *Monastery of Christ* and that I would be delighted to meet him. After I met Henri and realized how much fun it would be to go with him and Jorge to Jalapa, I let go of my concerns and invited Henri to go with us to Jalapa. He said, "Yes!"

The next day at dawn, all of us piled into four rickety buses and headed off for what turned out to be an eight-hour trip. Jorge, Henri and I sat in the front of our bus. They chattered in Spanish most of the way, while I tried to follow. I tried to relax and hoped Greta and Kyria would forgive me for going. I could not help being anxious about hitting a land mine, for I had heard of several people who had been killed that way on roads outside Managua. That is why, when we boarded our bus, I noticed with a touch of guilt and relief that we were not the first in line. This meant we would not be likely to set off a mine.

We arrived in Jalapa late that afternoon, greeted by thunder, lightning and pouring rain. Right away, we went to a town meeting hall, built like a stage in the round, where Jorge was called on to speak once again. He stood in the center and led us in cheers as the local people joined in, "No pasarán" (they won't get through, referring to the Contras), and "El pueblo unido jamás será vencido" (the people united will never be defeated!). Jorge had boundless energy, while I felt near exhaustion. My body was weaving from fatigue, and I would have fallen had companions standing on both sides not held me up.

Since he understood the complexities of Nicaragua better than most of us, and since he spoke English and Spanish equally well, Jorge became our leader and group speaker. While I was proud of him, I also teased him by calling him Jesus Christ Superstar. Sometimes, I wanted him to just be ordinary like the rest of us, instead of so much in demand.

That night, we slept in two public high school buildings located within sight of contra mortar emplacements. Our hosts gave each of us one thin blanket, then placed the women in two

118

Buses to Jalapa

The mothers from whom we all asked forgiveness

The school buildings where we spent the night in Jalapa

Soldiers on the border above the schools

Defensive trenches dug by Sandinista soldiers

Our group displaying banners

empty schoolrooms and the men in two others. It was cold on those concrete floors. I wanted to cuddle closer to the woman next to me, but I hesitated. I was one of the first to get up to put on more clothes. Then, I heard local musicians playing parts of the *Misa Campesina* (peasant mass) outside on the basketball court. I went out. The music set me afire. I could not keep from dancing, but I didn't want people to think I was showing off, so I danced on the side. When Henri Nouwen noticed, he pulled me into the center and said, "Give your dancing to God!" So I did.

After mass and breakfast, mothers of Sandinista soldiers met us on the basketball court, then took us to the place where their sons, brothers and husbands had recently been killed. They were distraught, not only because they had lost their sons, but because the Contras had cut the bodies into pieces so they could not be buried whole. The local people believe that a person's dismembered body cannot be received in heaven. It was distressing to find U.S. bullet cartridges on the ground, cartridges which we assumed the Contras had left during one of their earlier attacks. At that point, we felt that all we could do was to ask these women for their forgiveness and symbolically protect them from more bloodshed by making a human chain between Jalapa and the Honduran border. One by one, members of our group asked the mothers to forgive us for allowing our government to do so much harm. They immediately forgave us. We had the impression they were doing what we found everywhere in Nicaragua; they were distinguishing between the government and the people of the United States. However, the fact that our government is elected by the people made it hard for me accept their generosity.

During our bus trip back to Managua, I kept thinking of the odds – a tiny country of hardly more than three million people was facing the most powerful country in the world. The only hope for them was for the truth to be publicized. I wished that the things we were seeing might be reported in reputable newspapers. I thought of my great-grandfather, Adam Bridge, and wished that a reporter who told the truth to promote justice, as he did, might have been with us. Instead, most U.S. newspaper reports left people believing that the U.S. government was justified in backing the killers in order to stop communism.

I had just learned that Ray Bonner, a reporter who covered Central America, had recently been transferred from his Latin American post on the *New York Times* staff. Afterwards, I heard that his transfer occurred because the *Wall Street Journal* (February 10, 1982) and State Department officials had criticized him. They questioned the veracity of his report of the El Mozote massacre, which occurred in El Salvador on December 10, 1981. The *United Nations Truth Commission* later revealed that this was the biggest massacre of the entire war. Approximately seven hundred people were killed by a U.S. trained Salvadoran army battalion. To get this story straight from Ray Bonner, I called him in Vienna in mid-July 1997. He spoke of himself in the third person:

> Criticism from the *Wall Street Journal* and the Reagan administration had an impact on Bonner's career. There were editors at the paper who were concerned about his reporting. Eventually, he was pulled out of Central America and put on the business beat. That was a very sensitive time. It is hard to recall so long ago. We were reliving the fifties. Everybody was afraid of being seen as soft on communism. Congress had no balls.

The transfer of Ray Bonner and other incidents signaled to correspondents that they needed to write in such a way that for every atrocity of the Salvadoran military or of the Contras, there had to be an equal number reported from the other side. This was a totally inaccurate way of telling the story. There was no balance between those whom the U.S. supported and the other side. For example, the *U.N Truth Commission for El Salvador* registered more than twenty-two thousand complaints of seri-

ous acts of violence that occurred in El Salvador between January 1979 and July 1991. Those giving testimony attributed
almost eighty-five percent of the cases of forced disappearances,
executions and torture to agents of the military and the death
squads. Salvadoran insurgents were accused in approximately
five percent of the cases (*From Madness to Hope,* The Report of
the *U.N. Truth Commission,* page 43.)

On the fourth of July, all 150 of us attended mass in the
church of Santa María de Los Angeles in Managua. Guitarists
played, and we danced with whole families, many of whom
were members of *base ecclesial communities.* We rejoiced with
them not only for their "triumph" over the Somoza regime, but
also for their victories in establishing education, health and job-
training programs to benefit the majority of the people. As in
Jalapa, Nicaraguans in Managua did not wait to celebrate until
the war ended, but kept on praying and dancing, even as they
faced enormous odds. Toward the end of the service, Tomás
Borge, Minister of the Interior, showed up to thank us for
coming, and at the end said, "Me loves you!"

Afterwards, leaders of our group spoke with him and other
Sandinista leaders once again about establishing an international presence along the border. At first, Borge reiterated what he
had said before, "Definitely not. We do not want any of you to
be killed!" However, the Sandinista leaders finally agreed, and
plans for *Witness for Peace* began that summer in 1983. Americans would be sent to dangerous places like Jalapa to use their
bodies as a protection for the Nicaraguan people.

On the way home from that trip, Jorge and I spent a few days
with his family in Mexico City. He showed me the tiny two-
room apartment where he had lived together with his mother,
his brother and his sister from the time he was ten until he was
fourteen years old. He said his mother was one of the few in
that tenement building who had not succumbed to prostitution
or selling drugs to survive. After seeing that small apartment,

124

Some of us went back to Managua by truck.

Tomás Borge

*Henri Nouwen with children during mass
at the Church of Santa Maria de Los Angeles.*

Henri and Jorge in prayer at the mass

126

Guitarists playing in the church of Santa Maria de Los Angeles.

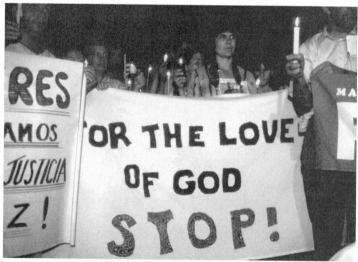

*A July fourth demonstration held at
the American Embassy in Managua*

located in a barrio of downtown Mexico City, I had lots of dreams about Houston and my own home. Perhaps my unconscious was struggling to reconcile our different beginnings. Following that trip, I knew I wanted to be with Jorge and hoped we could bring our lives together. When we said good-bye at the Mexico City airport, he on his way to Atlanta and I to Austin, I was so in love that I missed my plane after telling him good-bye.

When I have found ways to commit myself to live unselfishly, as I did when I was working to stop the war in Central America, I have often been surprised by joy. How else would I have met my beloved Jorge, or spent eight hours on a bus with Henri Nouwen, or danced with Nicaraguan people in the *Church of Santa María de Los Angeles?* My life has been blessed time after time by surprises like these.

This is the hallway in the tenement apartment house in Mexico City where Jorge lived as a teenager

Soon after that trip in July 1983, Buck Arnold sent me a copy of the telegram that he had sent to Senator Bentsen:

> Someone, in whom I have great confidence, has recently returned from Central America and reports that people are committing atrocities actively supported by the U.S. I rely upon you and others in Washington to know the facts and work the best solution possible for our country. However, I do pray we never permit the use of inhumane acts no matter what.

A telegram like this from Buck meant more than one hundred letters from those of us who did not have such strong connections in Washington. But Bentsen's reply was hard for me to believe. He told Buck that as far as he knew no such atrocities were being committed and that if he found out they were, he would stop them.

It helped our cause that Kyria was then serving as an intern to Senator Bentsen as part of her work at Madeira School in Virginia. When I went to see her, I visited with Senator Bentsen and his aide, who subsequently became my friend. The aide told me during one of my visits that large numbers of church people were coming to Washington to report their opposition to the government's involvement in Central America, and that their testimonies were beginning to get legislators' attention. He admitted to me that Reagan's "evidence" regarding the Sandinista's delivery of military equipment to the Salvadorean insurgents was questionable.

After my return from that trip, I received this note from the aide, written on July 5, 1985:

> I am certain you realize that one of the more frustrating aspects of this work is that one's personal positions are not always entirely congruent with the policies expounded by one's employer. It was extremely refreshing to have your insights and to feel the enthusiasm of your commitment.
>
> I hope you have a safe and successful visit in Nicaragua.

> There is a possibility that I too will be traveling in the
> region later this summer and, if so, I will make it a point to
> have you brief me prior to my departure.

As Bentsen's aide had indicated, church people from all over the U.S. were keeping up the pressure on their legislators. We can't prove it, but I do believe the U.S. government would have taken much more drastic measures to destroy the work of the Sandinistas if church groups had not spoken out.

Those days, it took courage for anyone to speak out. As Ray Bonner said, "We were all afraid of being seen as soft on communism." To be seen as friendly to the people in Nicaragua or El Salvador would have been to experience what it was like to be a social pariah. No one chooses to be alienated from friends or cause problems for their own children, least of all me. That is why it was agonizing for me to stand up for strangers in Central America at a time when the climate in our country was riddled with fears of communism. Many times, I felt isolated in my church and from some of my friends – at times even from my own daughters.

Nevertheless, I knew it would have been cowardly for me to remain silent. In 1983, after returning from my second trip to Nicaragua, I told the parents of one of Greta's friends what we had seen. Later, her friend's dad said he thought I might be a communist. For my sake and for Greta's, I hated those accusations. It felt so unfair for people to hint that I might be a communist when my fervor grew out of my concern that we, of all countries in the world, should deal justly with others.

I had a similar experience when the parents of Greta's wonderful boyfriend came to dinner. Just as I was thinking what a good time we were having, the father said, "Why take the Maryknoll nuns seriously? They are all communists!"

I silently remembered the Maryknoll sisters in El Salvador who in 1980 had been ambushed in their car on the road near the airport, raped, and killed by orders from the Salvadoran

military (*New York Times*, April, 1998). At that moment my friendship with the parents of Greta's boyfriend seemed more
important than being outspoken.

As I became more active, Greta felt more pressured. She was
criticized for my forthrightness and wanted to be seen as the
daughter of "normal parents." It was terribly unfair for her to
bear that burden, but I did not believe it would help her for me
to silence my conscience. While she respected my work, I knew
she was uneasy. Jorge and I were concerned about her feelings,
but we saw no way to protect her from the repercussions of
our commitments.

When Greta chose to write her senior paper (in 1985) on
the U. S. government's role in Nicaragua, Jorge and I were
delighted and helped her get the facts. Then, when her work
was completed, we saw that she came out in support of the
U.S. government policies. We didn't understand until twelve
years later, when she explained that this had been her way of
achieving "balance." She thought that showing us the other
side might widen our understanding and also make our family
appear to have a "balanced position." Both Jorge and I were
grateful when she said recently, "Mama, I always respected the
way you stood up for what you believed while most of my
friends' parents didn't seem to care. And I appreciated you and
Jorge even more when, years later, I learned that everything
you were saying turned out to be true."

One week after Greta graduated from *St. Stephen's* (in 1986),
Jorge and I were married in our Austin home. Judith Liro
came into the bedroom with me. While I got dressed, she put
the final touches on the prayers she would give in the ceremony. Then, I simply walked out of my bedroom with my
beloved friend Bonnie Bain, and stood at one end of our living
room, where we got married. As I knelt on the step and said
my vows, I held Jorge's hand as tightly as I could. Tears were
choking me, perhaps because, this second time, I knew how

Jorge and me at our wedding

momentous it was to commit myself forever. It comforted me
to see my dad behind me sitting on the long bench at the end
of the room between Greta and Buck Arnold. It also comforted
me to see our cleaning lady, Arfelia, who had adopted me as
her grandchild, sitting on a step in the living room holding
Kyria's hand. It meant a great deal to me to be surrounded by
five members of my new Mexican family, whom I have come
to cherish. I will never forget the tender look on Jorge's sister's
face, letting me know I had become her sister forever. Mother
is the one I missed. In the same way that she always encouraged my independent spirit, she would have given Jorge and
me her blessing. At the end of the ceremony, five ministers, one
Catholic, one Lutheran, two Presbyterian, and one Episcopa-
lian, all laid their hands on us while Judith Liro led us in prayer.
After we were blessed, mariachis began to play, and we broke
out in dancing.

That very night, after our guests left, the telephone rang. An
official from the *World Council of Churches* in Geneva asked Jorge if
he could be in San Salvador the next day to negotiate with
Salvadoran government leaders. A few days before, fifteen
Salvadoran church activists had been jailed. It was alleged that
they had been bringing food, medicine and weapons to Salvadoran insurgents. People accused the activists, saying they had
obtained money from international church agencies, money
that had been ear-marked for emergency refugee assistance.
Jorge asked me how I felt about his going away so quickly. I
hesitated, but I also felt honored to participate, even indirectly,
in something so close to my heart, and I told him to go ahead.
Two days later, Jorge and the other church leaders met with
President Duarte. They appealed to his Christian conscience,
and the captives were freed.

I met Jorge at the Houston Airport when he returned, and
we drove immediately to Crockett where I was meeting with
my siblings, nieces, and nephews for a business conference.

Jorge had never met my brother and sister, so I warned him they would probably have little interest in hearing about his trip. Even then, it was a blow to him when they did not respond to any of his accounts. They knew little about the war in Central America and did not care about what was going on there. Jorge's feelings mattered a lot to me, but I was used to their attitude and I could partially separate myself from them.

While Greta and Kyria were not indifferent to what was happening in Central America, their generation did not believe so totally in the American dream as did ours. They were not so shocked to learn about the United States government's role in Central America. I was a child during our "glorious victory" over Hitler in World War II, but Kyria and Greta grew up during the Vietnam War days. For them, the United States may never have been "the promised land," as it was for me. The land of Pilgrims and Puritans, the land of dreams for the oppressed everywhere, was disappearing for so many, including me. I began to see the U.S. government as more like the Egypt from which Moses had fled than the land of "milk and honey" to which he led the Israelites. But, like the Hebrews of antiquity, the Nicaraguans had caught glimpses of a new land, a place where people were inspired to care for their neighbors, to forgive their enemies, to educate the illiterate and heal the sick.

In spite of the overwhelming obstacles, I was hopeful. After all, it was groups of Americans who started the *Witness for Peace* in Nicaragua and, as Lloyd Bentsen's aide had said, many American church people were beginning to speak out in Washington. Yes, my American dream had been shattered, but I still believed that if people here only knew what was going on, they would make our government stop. After all, it was our government.

8

We See Through the Camouflage

During the 1980's, it was hard to see through the camouflage. Claims that communism was spreading throughout Central America and that Nicaragua was becoming another Cuba were broadcast loud and often. I wanted to do my part in piercing the screen of misinformation so Americans could see what was really happening. To do this, I knew funding would be essential.

My first effort was to set up a small charitable fund late in 1981. Called *Hospitalidad-Austin*, the purpose of this fund was to help Salvadoran refugees who were fleeing the violence in El Salvador. Many refugees had walked all the way through Mexico, hoping to find protection in the United States. After crossing the border, they were apprehended and placed in detention centers like El Corralón, near Brownsville, in south Texas.

I worked with a group of church people who paid bail for a few refugees among the hundreds who had been detained. We chose the refugees whom we would support partly based on their ability to earn a living. After we paid their bail, averaging around $450 each, they were released. When it became obvious to me that I was not addressing my larger goal, which was to stop the U.S. government from contributing to the violence in Central America, I decided to change my focus.

In 1982, I told Buck Arnold I wanted to start a foundation

with my modest savings of twenty thousand dollars. This could be added to the five thousand remaining in the *Hospitalidad-Austin* fund. Buck completed the necessary legal work in the summer of 1983. The first purpose of this foundation, which I named *Expanding Horizons*, was to help make more American people aware of the role the United States was playing in Central America.

While Buck was doing the legal work, my Episcopal priest friend, Frank Sugeno, and I were brainstorming about how, with limited resources, we could encourage others to learn about our country's misplaced involvement in Central America. I was relieved when Frank told me how important it was not to generalize our efforts. Though our monthly lunch gatherings, prayer vigils, and lectures in Austin had enabled us to build a well-informed local group, we were having no real impact on the overall problem. Frank was right. It was time to move on to a more focused plan.

My friend, Frank Sugeno

We all agreed that the real obstacle to slowing the bloodshed was the passivity of most Americans. Jorge put the problem in a nutshell when he said, "The destruction caused by good people who are indifferent and uninformed can more than equal the evil of people with bad intentions." Before going to the library to help Kyria with her model U.N. assignment, I had been like one of those "good people" – indifferent and uninformed. Frank and I realized that as long as the majority of Americans remained unaware, our government's policy would continue. This time our efforts were focused. Our plan was to invite Episcopal and other church leaders to go to Central America, where they could see the realities with their own eyes.

Therefore, the first work of the Expanding Horizons' board was to organize and support these non-partisan fact-finding trips. Board members asked my good friend Mike Conroy, who had spent years working in Central America, to help set up these trips for church leaders. Mike's experience in academia and in the field made him the ideal person for this job.

It was a stretch for me, a nobody in the Episcopal Church, to call every single bishop, priest and church leader suggested by Frank Sugeno and others. I was encouraged when a number of community and church leaders responded positively. One of the first people to say yes was Paul Moore, the Episcopal Bishop of New York. He, in turn, asked to bring his good friend who was a lawyer on the board of the Wall Street Journal and various other newspapers. Several priests from New York and the northeast also signed up.

Our planning bore fruit. The first trip, in January 1984, worked out well. Between 1984 and 1987, *Expanding Horizons* and the *Central America Resource Center* together sent some thirty-five prominent church leaders from Episcopal, Methodist, Catholic, Lutheran and Presbyterian churches to visit El Salvador, Nicaragua and Honduras. Two Episcopal bishops went, several Episcopal priests, a Lutheran pastor, a Catholic priest, a

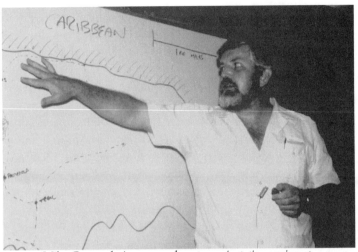

*Mike Conroy during our predeparture orientation session at
the Episcopal Seminary of the Southwest in Austin, Texas*

Jorge speaking at the orientation

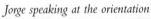

Catholic nun and several other Protestant and Catholic church leaders. All three trips (1984, 1985, and 1987) included visits to representatives from the full political spectrum in the countries visited. Participants saw American ambassadors, local church leaders, and members of the press and political groups who together represented all views.

Expanding Horizons paid for the full day orientation sessions, held at the *Episcopal Seminary of the Southwest* in Austin. Experts in the areas of religion, economics, politics and history led the presentations. Participants paid their own travel and lodging expenses. *Expanding Horizons* covered community meals and special events.

I participated in only one of these fact-finding trips. That was in 1985. Before, during, and after that 1985 trip to Central America, which included visits to Honduras, El Salvador and Nicaragua, I interviewed some of the trip participants. During this trip, I also found opportunities to interview families in Nicaragua and El Salvador. Lizzie Boyle, from Washington D.C., was the first person from our group whom I interviewed. She had been a nurse, was an active participant in her Episcopal church's Bible study group and was a mother of two children. She was married to a Washington D.C. banker. On our way to El Salvador, I asked her if she was frightened. She replied:

> I'm a little bit frightened about going down and finding that Americans are terrible, that our American policy has always been bad. I don't want to find that, although I know I will. So I'm in a battle, because I care very much about America. I know it is partly guilt that is driving me, because I'm forty-two years old and it was my generation that went into Vietnam. Some of my classmates were actually killed there, and I don't want that to happen again.

Like so many of us, Lizzie hated to find out the truth, yet she had the courage to look.

Then I spoke with Dot Ettling, a sister of the *Incarnate Word*

Community and president of her Catholic women's religious congregation, which had about eight hundred members. She was also the principal of *Incarnate Word High School*, the president of *Incarnate Word University*, and the superintendent of *Santa Rosa Hospital*, all in San Antonio, Texas. When I asked her what she hoped for, she replied:

> I hope to become better informed. I don't pretend that we'll be experts after this amount of time, but there will be opportunities to meet with people and hear and see some of the reality that will make us better informed. I also hope to build a sense of solidarity with the people there who, I think, are suffering a lot.

When I asked if she were scared, she said,

> I'm less frightened for my safety than what it will do to me personally, especially to my sense of responsibility and my frustration afterwards, because I think that's very real.

John Pyle, the canon pastor at the National Cathedral, in Washington D.C., a member of the *Washington Peace Commission*, father and grandfather, explained why he wanted to go:

> I hope it is going to be illuminating, for I really feel a great need to sort out that situation, in effect, to have more ammunition to respond to people in Washington who raise questions one way or the other about the political situations in Central America.... I also want in some way to make this trip a small symbol of support for people who are in Central America.

I asked him what made him so different from Americans who were not interested in going, and he said:

> I just have what I would take to be some of the concerns of a Christian citizen about people who are in situations where they're confronted by various oppressions and injustices. I do feel that there is, somewhere down in the Biblical fundamentals of the faith, a requirement that we concern ourselves with the cause of justice for people. I want to be

Liz Boyle

John Pyle with Sister Dot Ettling

Jim Lewis

better prepared to do that.

In response to the question regarding what frightened him, Jim Lewis, an Episcopal priest, married with four children, and an ex-U.S. Marine, said:

> I'm very nervous about El Salvador. I expect I'll find a very repressive situation there. But, I expect to be welcomed in Nicaragua. The irony of it is, I don't have much fear about Nicaragua, except being shot by one of our bullets. In El Salvador, which has basically become our country (in that we have taken it over), I have a lot of hesitation.

Jim was right about both countries, especially El Salvador. There, fear filled the air..

In El Salvador, it often seemed that we were being watched. We even wondered if our lodgings were bugged. One time, after we had eaten breakfast downstairs in the hotel, two people in our group found things scattered about in their room. Their room had been searched. That same day, I went for a walk. When a woman passed me on the street, I asked, "Como está?", (How are you?) She replied, "Tengo miedo," (I'm scared). That's how we felt too.

One morning we visited with the *Mothers of the Disappeared, Imprisoned and Murdered of El Salvador.* Visiting "the mothers" made me see the oppression under which so many Salvadoran people lived. As we reached the top of the narrow stairway leading to the office, a tiny woman with her hair pulled back took both my hands in hers, put her face next to mine and said, "We are so grateful you've come." Other "mothers," young and old, arranged folding metal chairs in a circle. We sat with them, listened and watched the pain in their faces as they told us stories of their children who had been taken by the National Police and had never returned. Francisca's story was typical:

> The National Police came late at night in 1981, took my son in his underwear and me too, in their Cherokee to their office. They then let me go. I returned every day for seven-

teen days asking for him. They told me to leave or they would arrest me too. My brother went to protest. They told him to get out or they would kill him. I never saw my son again. I joined "the mothers." Last month my twenty-one year old daughter was killed. I have her child who is two.

Dot Ettling at the meeting of the Mothers of the Disappeared, (notice Archbishop Romero's face imprinted on her apron).

Such testimony made it clear to me why the first woman I met in El Salvador said her life was filled with fear. If Greta or Kyria had "been disappeared" by the police, people whom I count on to protect me, I would have been tempted to give up. I admired the spirit of those mothers.

A visit with the auxiliary bishop of San Salvador, Gregorio Rosas, showed us what was happening on a larger scale. He spoke about the insurgents as people with whom one could reasonably negotiate:

> I believe the reason they took up arms was that they were "up to here" with what has been happening. In 1932, when the rural poor rose in protest because their lands had been taken and many were jobless, around 30,000 were killed by the military. Our Pope, John Paul II, told us in 1982 that our problems are from social injustice more than anything else. Though some leaders of the opposition are Marxist, eighty percent of the fighters are Christians, really Christians. Would anyone ask if the American revolutionaries were terrorists?

From news accounts in the U.S. at that time, one would have concluded that "Marxist Guerillas" were maliciously destroying entire communities. Anyone not in agreement with the government was labeled a communist and subject to legalized murder. Under those guidelines, not even decent, ordinary citizens of any social class were safe. Those days, in El Salvador, the only people who were safe were the military and super rich. I wanted to find out for myself if middle-class Christians were being targeted. If so, that would establish that practically no one was safe. It would also support Bishop Rosas' statement that many of the people opposed to the military government were Christians.

During the 1984 trip, I wanted to find a Protestant middle-class family in San Salvador that I might interview. Soon after we arrived in San Salvador, Jorge and I visited the *Emmanuel*

Marta and Cheque Castro in the Baptist Church in San Salvador

Baptist Church, where we met Cheque and Marta Castro. Marta, dressed as she was in a black-and-white polka-dot cotton dress, with her bright smile and short, curly black hair, would have blended into any church group in the U.S. Her story would not. After church, I asked the Castros if they would consent to being interviewed by me in their home. They readily agreed.

After dinner that evening, we drove to their comfortable home, built by Cheque, who was a professional builder. Marta volunteered to be interviewed first. We went into a bedroom down the hall from the living room. When I asked her about her hopes, she said:

> My hopes have always been to have a happy home, a hope shared by most women. I have always wanted this for my husband and five sons. However, this has not been possible. Since the problems began here, my sons have suffered a lot. José (a teenager then) was tortured. We could not under-

Marta Castro at her home in San Salvador

stand why, because he was not involved in any political organization on the right or the left.

I asked her what happened and she said:

In his spare time, he volunteered to help with an emergency task force established by our church in 1981. José transported food to needy people. Soldiers picked him up on the highway. They accused him of taking these supplies to the subversives. They covered his eyes and threatened to kill him if he would not admit to being the leader. When he refused, they took him to a strange place and covered his head with a *capuchon* (a hood covering his head). This treatment is something well known to Salvadoreans. They then beat him.

I asked Marta where she got her strength:

> From God, as I have since I was a child. I was raised in a
> Protestant church home which taught me to turn to God,
> for He would respond. As a mother and a daughter of God,
> I have also taught my sons that when we do not help others,
> we are rejecting the Lord himself. This is why we believe
> that even in the middle of this anguish, we, as Christians
> have a commitment. Where there is suffering and pain, God
> calls for us to be a consolation and hope for others. Think-
> ing of others' needs has strengthened my life.

I wondered how she helped others in her work. She explained:

> I work mainly with poor women who need to learn skills
> like how to prepare a meal inexpensively. Some are so poor,
> they cannot eat. We also teach them to sew their own
> clothes and to know the Lord. Then they teach others what
> they learn.

Next, I interviewed her husband, Cheque. He was a short man
with wide shoulders topped by a large head. As he came into
the room for the interview, he looked ready to begin an important task. He sat down on the bed opposite me. His hands were
trembling. He held the tape recorder microphone as if it were a
holy instrument. When I asked what he hoped for, his words
poured out:

> If the question is what do I hope for my town, well, I hope
> for peace. But there are strong men who are making sure
> there is no peace. However, the strongest is God. If people
> in the United States are Christians, as they claim to be, and
> if they believe in God as they say, then why don't they stop
> sending the armaments, which are being used to kill people
> in El Salvador? We do not want money. We want jobs. We
> want to find a piece of land.

> We pray that these things will be worked out without
> violence, without destroying the people who are left here.
> Some of them are cripples.

> We do not want charity, but we do want to be able to talk
> freely, even shout freely. The truth is we can not do that
> now.

> Now, the way things are, even the poorest janitor in the
> United States has more power over our country than we,
> ourselves.

The violence inflicted on the people by the military in El Salvador and the money sent by the United States to pay for it were
both camouflaged. What we saw during our visit to Tenancingo,
a town outside San Salvador, gave us a glimpse of this camouflage. Tenancingo was mostly deserted, because the people had
fled when it was occupied by the military. As we walked to the
little school right outside the town, soldiers at arms length
from me were so camouflaged I hardly noticed them. Both in
the U.S. and in El Salvador, the real truth was hidden so that
few people could see what was really happening. Noticing
combinations of visible and invisible camouflage in Tenancingo
inspired me to write this poem:

Camouflaged

Late one afternoon this November,
   I walked outside Tenancingo
      toward the children's school.
   The road was quiet.
   Banana and coffee trees
      covered the cliff on my left.

First, I saw one, then another and another
   standing like the trees,
      leaved limbs in their boots,
   belts and collars.
One, right beside me – I could have touched him.
   His left foot planted in the ditch
      and his right on the incline
   He held the black barreled gun close,
      hid it with his body.

I looked at his boyish face darkened with smudge
and wondered who gave him orders.

"Things are better," they say.

Death squads are careful.
Torturers leave no mark.
They come at night dressed in civies,
driving a Cherokee with dark windows.
They stop the minister,
yank him from his car,
leave his child
and three parishioners in the dark.
Black plastic over his head,
they beat him, one, two, three, four, five
days –
interrogation, no sleep.
His family cannot find him.
What's his crime?
He directs relief to the hungry.

"Those poor help the guerrillas," they say.

Only Communists do that.
Are there Communists in the plastic huts
we saw in San Salvador?

The earth quakes.
Walls break.
Hungry mothers and children
show through the camouflage.

Just before leaving San Salvador in 1985, we met with a friend
of Jorge's, Jon Sobrino, a Jesuit theologian and professor at the
Catholic University of San Salvador, who confirmed what some of
us had learned. He told us:

> The cause of this war is poverty, real poverty, which means
> being near to death, not poverty as we know it. The poorest
> people do not say, "We want communism, we want to live."
> They only say, "We want to live." In order to live, they

Jon Sobrino, Jesuit theologian

organize a bit. Then, they are killed violently.

Their poverty is an institutional sin. The first step is to ac-
knowledge this fact, not cover it up with phrases like, "We
are on the road to democracy." That further hides the reality.
The United States should realize our country and others
like it need radical change. That should not threaten the
United States. They have enough resources to help these
countries so they will not go to the far left. Why don't they
talk with the insurgents? Why aren't they able to show
more creativity?

I appreciated Sobrino's emphasis on the United States' effort to
cover up its actions by seductive words. As I listened to him, I
made the connection between words used to hide dark actions
and the Salvadoran boy soldiers' camouflage – made to blend

into the trees in Tenancingo. Also, I agreed with Jon's reference to "institutional sin," because it showed me that even if we do not pull triggers, we can still maim and kill. From Sobrino, I learned that I am still guilty even if I do nothing, because to do nothing is ultimately not so different from doing the killing myself.

According to Sobrino's concept of institutional sin, we Americans certainly were not innocent! During the 1980's, the U.S. was training whole battalions of the Salvadoran army at the *School of the Americas* in Fort Benning, Georgia. Between 1979 and 1991 our government sent the government of El Salvador over six billion dollars, mostly for the military. (The U.N. Report of the Commission on the Truth for El Salvador, page xviii, *Promised Land, Death and Life in El Salvador*, Orbis Books, New York 1993) By 1985, over sixty thousand Salvadoran non-combatants had been killed in a country of approximately five million people. Over one million, or one-fifth of the people, were homeless.

It was a relief to leave El Salvador and move on to Nicaragua. Liz Boyle echoed the feelings of our whole group as she compared our experiences in El Salvador and Nicaragua:

> I left the country (El Salvador) just sick, so angry with the duplicity of the American government, all in the name of democracy. ... I'd heard all sorts of dreadful stories about how oppressed the Nicaraguan people were from our family friend who works in the State Department [referring to John Negroponte, the U.S. ambassador to Honduras at that time]. In fact, we found exactly the opposite. We were elated. You could talk freely. The whole attitude of the country was upbeat, courageous. People were working together. They weren't working against the government. Everything that was happening was in the open. The work those people are doing is a joyous thing, and they could be an example to the world if this government could be allowed to grow without outside interference.

During the Nicaraguan portion of our fact-finding trip, Mike Conroy took the group up to the Honduran border while Jorge and I went to visit the Laras whom I had met during my first trip to Nicaragua. This time I interviewed the Lara family, beginning with Dr. Lara. He explained why, as a doctor, he was very pleased about the accomplishments of the Nicaraguan people:

> Before the revolution in 1979, only a few were rich. Now we have a society in which the poor are favored. Previously, as many as fifty people lived in one house without minimal living conditions. Now many Nicaraguans are living like people for the first time. There are programs for housing, health, education and agrarian reform. Previously, medical treatment was a luxury. Now, it is available to all.

> Nicaragua is a free nation, sovereign and independent. I also think the U.S. is free, sovereign and independent. I wonder what North Americans would think if Nicaragua intervened in the political affairs of the U.S.?

In battling to defend Nicaragua from the Contras, the Nicara-

Dr. Valentin and Mercedes Lara

guan people were up against great odds – the U.S. government. Valentín was very careful to make it clear that the destruction of their country was being propelled by the U.S. government and not by U.S. citizens. Neither he nor his family blamed us.

Like Cheque Castro, Valentín wanted to stop the United States from destroying his country, but he felt helpless in the face of so much power. He hated to see forty percent of the Nicaraguan national budget being used to defend the country from attacks by the Contras. This meant the health, education and housing programs had to be cut to the bone.

Next, I spoke with his wife, Mercedes. I have a clear memory of looking into her dark brown eyes set off by her ivory white face. She looked at me intently as she told me about her life:

> I am Mercedes Toruño de Lara. I am 44 years old, and have four children. We also have a young adopted daughter who comes from the war zone. She is a gift from God. My husband and my brother are both doctors. I am the coordinator of Christian community groups here.
>
> When we have a larger activity planned, we invite all the groups in this area. We just had the monthly mass for the eight mothers killed by the Contras. They were going to the border to visit their children. They were in a civilian vehicle. They were ambushed. Some were raped, mutilated, then killed. We, as a community-based group, offered a mass for them at the *Church of Mercy*. The whole town came.

Are you afraid Leon might be attacked?

> If we are attacked, our home will have to be closed so we can do our jobs. Valentín, as a doctor, has his work. Each of the children has a place in the trenches. I am responsible for my neighborhood defense committee. It is painful to imagine going home, then waiting to see who will return.

What gives you strength?

> Faith gives us our strength.

She then talked about her own work to rehabilitate former prostitutes by teaching them job skills.

The Lara's son, Pedrarias, had just returned from six months at the battlefront where he and fifteen other professors had volunteered to care for the wounded. I quote from an interview with him:

> Our equipment was poor compared to that of the Contras. For example, our blankets were not waterproof. When it rained, they got so heavy we had to throw them away. The Contras have plastic sleeping bags which zip up from the feet, so they are rested in the morning.

> We were up in the mountains of Nueva Segovia, near the border of Honduras. There, the Contras acted like murderers. Many people captured by Contras were brutalized. They cut off their testicles, then slit their abdomens with bayonets. I saw the bodies of some of the men in my group

The Lara Family — back: Alberto Lara, Magali Lara, Dr. María Eugenia Lara & Dr. Predarias Dávila; front: Dr. Valentín Lara, Hipolita Lara, Mercedes Lara, & Dr. Javíer Lara.

who had been wounded during a fight. The Contras had inserted bayonets through their eyes. When the Contras pass through an area, it is like a disaster passing through. Not only soldiers but citizens are afraid of the day when the Contras may come. They kill children, old people, any who are in their path.

After the interview, Pedrarias asked me to turn off the recorder and said sadly that he and María Eugenia had been married a year and were afraid to have children. They feared one day they could be killed, and their children would be left orphans.

Pedrarias did not exaggerate. By the time of this interview, in the mid-eighties, approximately 20,000 Nicaraguans had been killed, including doctors, teachers and agricultural technicians, who were specifically targeted. Schools, clinics, agricultural cooperatives and farms had been systematically destroyed. More than 270,000 people had been displaced from their homes, and the country had suffered at least 2.5 billion dollars worth of damage to its economy. (Fagen, Richard, *Forging Peace: The Challenge of Central America*, published by Pacca, 1987, page 59).

Magali and María Lara with a banner they made:
"Christ Lord of life Strengthen our hope in the face of aggression"

The work of the Nicaraguan people and of the Sandinistas had been practically ruined by the Contras, the people President Reagan called "Freedom Fighters." How could we, as a nation, stand for freedom and still find it acceptable to interfere in the lives of the Nicaraguans for so many years? Perhaps it was because people like me had not bothered to find out what was happening.

Nicaraguan elections in November of 1984 confirmed what we had seen with our own eyes – that the work being done by the Sandinistas in Nicaragua was about rebuilding their country, not about being surrogates for communism. These elections were recognized for their fairness by international delegations including Western European parliamentarians and United States academics. The Sandinistas won approximately sixty-seven percent of the votes, almost the same percentage that Reagan received in the U.S. election.

Seven parties participated, three to the right and three to the left of the Sandinistas. The three parties opposing the Sandinistas from the left were the Communist, Socialist and Marxist Leninist. Each of these groups won only two seats from a total of ninety-six in the National Assembly. These facts are taken from a document called *Report on the Nicaraguan Elections of November 4, 1984* (December, 1984, Washington Office on Latin America in Washington D. C.). That was significant, since the justification for the United States' policy of hostility against the Sandinistas was that they were Communists. Obviously, that policy was based on a fabrication.

In spite of the Sandinistas' election triumph in 1984, and the fact that over sixty percent of the Nicaraguan economy was in private hands, and that the life of the Nicaraguan people kept improving, President Reagan still claimed the Sandinistas were communists and should be demolished. He persuaded the U.S. Congress to send an additional one hundred million dollars in 1986 to support the Contras. Those of us who knew about the

successes and the struggles of the people in Nicaragua were aghast. The Nicaraguan people, from one of the tiniest countries in the world (around three and one-half million people), had an uphill battle, because the Contras, who were backed up by the most powerful country in the world, were tearing down Nicaragua faster than the people could build it up.
(Note: During this time period, it became clear that the U.S. was involved in the Iran/Contra dealings. The U.S. government secretly diverted to the Nicaraguan Contras millions of dollars from the illegal sale of military arms to Iran, a declared enemy of the U.S. ... It was also alleged that planes carrying arms to the Contras in Honduras returned to the U.S. with drugs, which were sold in the U.S. to buy more arms for the Contras. Those subjects are beyond the purview of my work here.)

After the U.S. Congress's decision in 1986, Mercedes Lara wrote to comfort us:

> Knowing that you, our friends in the United States, are suffering along with us, strengthens us. When the $100 million was approved to support the Contras, our first reaction was to write and say, "Be strong – the Lord will help us and you too. We are united in the same heart and in the Lord. Somehow, we must find the strength to construct the peace that will not fall ready-made from heaven."

We had danced with the Nicaraguans in Jalapa and Managua and had seen the fruits of their hard-won victories; now we were devastated. Seeing their dreams destroyed by our own government was heartbreaking.

Mercedes wrote to me on March 14, 1994, that María Eugenia and Pedrarias had a baby and that the baby had leukemia. She also said Valentín was profoundly depressed. He was discouraged that the Contras and their U.S. sponsors were destroying the accomplishments of the revolution. When we are faced with such tragedy and devastation, when people's dreams have momentarily been realized at great cost and then are trampled on, sometimes it seemed to me there was little we could do but weep.

Indeed many of us asked each other about how God could be present in the midst of so much suffering of innocent people. The answer frequently given by church people upsets me, "God is all powerful! Whatever happens is his will. Those people are suffering for a purpose. We must accept it." To affirm divine omnipotence would make God ultimately responsible for the evil and the good in the world.

Fortunately, Jesus reveals a different kind of God, one who loves, and for that very reason, forswears omnipotence in order to enable those whom he loves to love in return. I believe that the self-limitation of God implies that He/She needs our help in accomplishing the victory of good over evil.

9

We Break Through the Camouflage

Since the fact-finding trips to Central America, I have gotten in touch with some of the participants. I wanted to find out what they learned and if they were inspired to share it with others. A week after people returned from the first fact-finding trip, I called most of them. Michael Phillips and John Kater, then both clergy at Christ Episcopal Church in Poughkepsie, New York, were so taken aback by what they had seen in Nicaragua that on their return they immediately visited the offices of their senators, Alfonse D'Amato and Daniel Moynihan. Later, Hamilton Fish, the congressional representative from their district, came to their church for a lengthy meeting with both of them. Michael and John also set up a series of meetings to talk with people in their diocese about what they had seen. Later they met with a group of students from Vassar College.

In September 1997, John Kater told me that our fact-finding trip to Nicaragua in 1985 had changed his life. In February 1985, one month after returning from that trip, he was called by Bishop James Ottley, then Bishop of Panama, to serve as the Educational Officer for the Episcopal Church in Panama. John said, "I would not have been able to imagine doing that job if I had not just been primed by my trip to Nicaragua and Honduras. That trip gave me a chance to see what the possibilities for the church in Central America were."

For six years, John Kater trained approximately seventy-five lay people from all walks of life to serve in that diocese as priests and church leaders. In 1990 he began working at the *Church Divinity School of the Pacific* (the Episcopal seminary in Berkeley, California) where he now serves as professor of ministry development. His experience with the poor in Latin America inspired him to make "the marginalized" the center of his teaching at the divinity school. It gratified me to learn that the fact-finding trip had influenced him to put the poor in first place. In 1997 John was invited to lead the clergy conference of the *Episcopal Church of Panama* and was amazed to see that around fifteen members, or more than one-half of the clergy at the conference, had studied with him.

At the end of the 1985 fact-finding trip, I interviewed Jim Lewis:

> I remember seeing the nuns who were on the Nicaraguan side of the border with Honduras. I then looked up at a hillside and saw three wooden crosses, three bare wooden crosses, between their church and the border of Honduras. Across the street, I saw an Alka-Seltzer sign and thought what a headache we are to these people. I thought to myself how wrong this war is, and how courageous people like those nuns are who put their bodies between an oppressive force and the people being oppressed. To me, that's what the whole Christian faith is all about – putting your body between people and with people.

Much later, in the summer of 1996, he told me:

> My life changed radically as a result of my trip in 1985. It put flesh and blood on my commitment to Central America. A year after that trip, I moved to North Carolina, where I worked with the bishop in the *Episcopal Diocese of North Carolina*.

Jim went on to tell me he had worked with my friend Gail

Phares, who led my first trip to Nicaragua in 1983 (through *CITCA, Carolina Interfaith Task Force on Central America*). Jim worked with Gail to plan *The North Carolina Pilgrimages for Peace*. On these pilgrimages, people spend several days before Easter walking from city to city in North Carolina, talking about Central America at points along their route. "The whole purpose of these pilgrimages, which continue to this day" (1996) Jim explained, "is to raise people's awareness about Central America."

Dot Ettling was not drawn to international bridge-building as Jim Lewis was. Rather, her experience in Central America played a part in her decision to help women in poverty be more proactive in their lives by involving them in workshops. When I interviewed her in March 1997, she said:

> The trip to Central America had a profound effect on me. I had never before been in a country ravaged by war. In Honduras, I remember the stories of the way children were used by the troops, and the fear that that sort of "U.S. imperialism" was everywhere. I saw the meaning of violence and the meaning of domination in a way that very much moved me - particularly the effects on children.
>
> I saw that whoever "protects their own rights" and goes against the United States as Nicaragua did, does not have a chance. To me, this is the epitome of the worst in what I call the American patriarchal culture.

Like Dot Ettling, Lizzie Boyle kept her focus close to home. She worked with John Walker, the bishop of Washington D.C., to plan a three-day Episcopal clergy conference on Central America for approximately 120 priests and church leaders. It took place in Washington in 1987. The fact that the conference was held in the political decision-making center of our country and was led by Jorge, who was so knowledgeable about Central America, was enough to convince me that our work would be fruitful. As a result of that clergy conference, the diocese as a whole gave Central America far more attention, both in its missionary outreach and in its pastoral care for the larger community of Central Americans living in the Washington D.C. area. Clearly, our work had been worthwhile.

Soon after the clergy conference, John Pyle worked with Bishop Walker and the *Peace Commission of the Diocese of Washington, D.C.* to set up a companion relationship with Bishop Leo Frade and the Episcopal diocese of Honduras. In the late 1980's, people from Washington area churches began to visit Honduras and Bishop Frade visited Washington. In March 1998, Beverley Allison and Carlin Rankin, who were both volunteering time to work with companion projects, brought me up to date on more recent bridge-building work.

Since 1986, over two-hundred Honduran and American students have visited each other's countries in annual exchange projects, and twenty-five Episcopal churches in the *Diocese of Washington* have been engaged in outreach projects like *Our Little Roses*, in San Pedro Sula in Honduras. This is a school and orphanage for homeless newborns and children of single working mothers. With the help of a charitable trust fund, lay people in the Washington diocese raised $50,000 to build a new building that will enable *Our Little Roses* to serve around three-hundred children. In this center, the children's mothers learn about nutrition and birth control.

When I talked to John Pyle about the positive effects stemming from his work, he said, "The 1985 Central America fact-finding trip firmed up a concern for Central America in *The Washington Peace Commission*. Now the work has spread beyond our original dreams."

I wondered what had become of the link between Christianity and the American Dream. After 1983, I could no longer see it, certainly not in the light of the dominant theme in Scripture – God's emphasis on the poor. Jesus himself made the

poor the focus of his ministry at the very beginning, as is shown
by his choice of scripture when he spoke at the synagogue in
Nazareth, his hometown:

> He stood up to read, and the scroll of the prophet Isaiah was
> given to him:
>
> "The spirit of the Lord God is upon me,
>
>> because the Lord has anointed me;
>
> he has sent me to bring good news to the oppressed,
>
>> to bind up the brokenhearted,
>
> to proclaim liberty to the captives,
>
>> and release to the prisoners."   (Luke 4:16-19)

Far from bringing good news to the oppressed, as Jesus did, our
government was acting as the oppressor of the most vulnerable,
both in El Salvador and Nicaragua. It supported the worst kind
of violence to "save" them and us from communism. The great
tragedy is that after the peace accords, international communities
lost interest in El Salvador and Nicaragua, assuming that peace
meant well-being, when in fact those countries had been
devastated. To this day, both countries are still reeling from the
violence of the 1980's.

Although in Nicaragua the civil war formally ended in June
1990, many people – a majority of them former Contras –
remained armed, at least until the late 1990's, especially in the
rural areas. The standard of living has fallen back to a level below
the 1950's under the Somoza regime. Well over half the population still lives in poverty, and unemployment is massive in many
areas. Money spent on education and health has been drastically
cut in order to promote exports and to pay back the foreign debt.
While there seem to be forces intent on pushing back the clock,
Nicaraguans have gotten a taste of freedom and refuse to
return to the pre-1979 days. Since the peace accords ended

the civil war in El Salvador in 1992, the Salvadoran government has reduced the military by fifty percent and placed it under civilian control. Also, the former opposition force known as the *FMLN (Farabundo Marti National Liberation Front)* has been recognized as a legal political party and has become El Salvador's second largest political force. Although people are no longer dragged out of bed by the national police in the middle of the night, civil liberties are still circumscribed by political violence, repressive police measures, a mounting crime wave and right wing death squads. These conditions were still the norm, at least until the late 1990's.

In trying to change our government's stance toward Central America, I learned how important it is for us to look here, in America, for the causes of violence in Central America. As Cheque told me, janitors in the U.S., with their vote, had more power over El Salvador than he had in his own country. I saw it was essential for us in the United States to first "take the log out of our own eyes."

In the late 1980's, as the U.S. government's support of the violence in Central America diminished, Cheque and many others like him prepared me for my task at home. By using what seemed like a tiny bit of clout and then working with others to find solutions, I learned that every one of us here can make a difference. What we learned through our involvement with Central America in the 1980's would shape the work of *Expanding Horizons* in the 1990's.

10

Expanding Horizons in the Early Nineties

My involvement with Central America proved to me that it is realistic to aim for what looks impossible. In the decade of the nineties, *Expanding Horizons* more than once reached goals that originally appeared to be unattainable. What we aimed to do by giving priority to the most needy was to change the arrangements that hold people in poverty.

Because the violence in Central America had diminished in the early 1990's and there was no longer such a crucial need to continue the fact-finding trips, *Expanding Horizons* began looking for a new focus. A trip to Mexico in the spring of 1991 suggested some possibilities. During this trip, sponsored by the *Funding Exchange* in New York City, Jorge and I visited a housing project in a poor barrio in Mexico City. I wrote in my journal:

> I watched the women gathered in the patio on the bottom floor, as I stood beside the only bathroom for thirty people. A hole in the middle of that tiny room served as a drain for the shower. There was no mirror or hot water. I wondered how the women there could appear so well turned out. Afterwards, I climbed up to the third floor and met a twenty-one-year-old pregnant woman, who with her two-year-old son was surviving in a room with a partially caved-

in ceiling, a floor with holes, unprotected windows looking onto the street. And she had an abusive husband.

After visiting the tenement, I resolved to help that young woman and all the other people in that house. However, I discovered that a limitation in U.S. tax laws made it impossible. At first I was discouraged, but in the long run the restriction was positive for *Expanding Horizons*, because it pointed us back home, where we could have a stronger influence.

In 1991, instead of continuing to work outside the country, the directors of *Expanding Horizons* decided to focus on the Texas/Mexico border, a place of appalling suffering. When we met with John Henneberger, Director of the *Texas Low Income Housing Information Service*, he explained that thousands of people in South Texas are so desperate for housing that they build flimsy shacks out of cardboard. Many of these people work on farms throughout the United States during seasonal times but live in South Texas. He said that approximately 340,000 people live in *colonias* on the U.S. side of the nine hundred mile Texas/Mexico border. *Colonias* are unincorporated suburbs with dirt roads, often located on flood lands, places which frequently have no potable water or sewage systems.

He also told us that developers had been taking advantage of the people who tried to buy land and build houses there. Since many *colonia* residents do not speak English, they don't understand the contracts. In the early 1990's, the cost of a barren lot 80' by 180' was between $8,000 and $12,000 with 12 percent to 18 percent interest. And this price does not include hookups for water and sewage. This is hard for people who have seasonal jobs and average incomes of $6,500. What makes it harder are the steep penalties for late payments. While lawyers from *Texas Rural Legal Aid* and the Texas State Attorney General's office have been working together with colonia residents to change the existing situation, local developers have been selling lots on a contract for deed basis. This means that without a mortgage, the family purchasing the land is essentially a tenant until it makes the last payment. A developer can evict the family even if they miss only one payment after faithfully paying on their land for several years. The tenants then lose not only the money they have paid for the land but also improvements on that land, including their house.

We took a chance. In 1991, John Henneberger presented us with a proposal from a grass roots board called *Proyecto Azteca*, which is affiliated with the *United Farm Workers' Union*. Their headquarters are located in Hidalgo County near McAllen in the Texas Rio Grande Valley. In their proposal, they asked for sixteen thousand dollars to purchase materials to build one home.

Their plan was for seven families to build seven homes together – one for each family. One member from each of the seven families agreed to help with the first home even if they were unable to get funding to build the remaining six houses. The *colonia* residents' initiative and their commitment to help themselves and one another impressed us. These attitudes were basic to our criteria for funding. *Expanding Horizons* aims to start new projects and to jump into situations where we can make a big difference with small amounts of money. That is what happened with this first grant to *Proyecto Azteca*.

Expanding Horizons board members were hesitant at first. The amount was over half the original value of the foundation. We saw no possible way those people could build all seven houses. We weren't sure if all seven families would be willing to work on the first house if they had no assurance that they could also get their own homes. Though we were not certain that this grant would make a difference in the enormous problems faced by people all along the border, we felt we could count on the determination of the *colonia* people and on John Henneberger. His can-do spirit, his tenacity and dedication to the poor, impressed us. Frank Sugeno smiled, and said, "We can't be sure these people will get more money to build the other six homes, but at least our sixteen thousand dollars will build one home for one family. So let's do it." And we did.

After we gave the grant, I asked others to join with us in what Walter Wink, my theologian friend and adopted brother, called the "big prayer." This meant to pray for what we hoped would happen, instead of what we thought was possible. Sister Amalia Rios, who was then working with housing development projects in Austin and South Texas, Frank Sugeno, Jorge and I, together with our churches and prayer groups, prayed that this initial grant would spread to span the nine-hundred mile Texas/Mexico border.

With so little money, we did make a difference. Few foundations respond to projects not already supported by other reputable grantors. If *Expanding Horizons* had turned down *Proyecto Azteca's* request for startup costs, other foundations probably would not have dared to step in. However, once the building project got under way and the participants had something to show, they invited board members from the *Texas Department of Housing and Community Affairs (TDHCA)* for a visit. Those board members were impressed when they saw the family home-building project in action. Before the end of 1992, TDHCA and *McAuley Institute* lent *Proyecto Azteca* the money to buy materials for the other six homes and to refinance numerous lots. (*McAuley* is a faith-based organization that works nationwide with communities to build housing.) These loans removed the developers from at least some of the contracts.

Soon afterward, HUD provided funding to pay groups of men as they were building their own homes and to hire a skills-building coordinator who taught and paid the men as they were constructing the houses. This meant that all seven families would have a home when the work was done, and that one person from each family would have an additional skill so they could more easily be employed.

The role of *Expanding Horizons* was becoming increasingly clear. By working with *Proyecto Azteca,* we learned that our job was to assist people in working toward a solution identified by them. We were asking the people we worked with to make plans for us, the funders, instead of the other way around. This way of surrendering to them a real measure of control seemed to me, then and now, to be a concrete expression of love at work. We called this "the bottom up" way. The bottom up approach strengthened the communities we were working with and enhanced the people's dignity. The remedies they had chosen lasted, because they were in charge.

Some time during our years of supporting community and house-building in South Texas, I wrote a new description of our work, which served as an informal mission statement:

> *Expanding Horizons* is a foundation whose priority is to address human suffering by supporting community efforts among the economically disadvantaged people in Texas. This foundation serves as a catalyst. It gives seed money to community-based groups to remedy the causes of problems, as identified by those groups, rather than focusing on symptoms. We seek innovative projects with the strength to become self-supporting and the potential for spreading.

Early in 1992, *Expanding Horizon* board members visited a *Proyecto Azteca* board meeting, held in the *United Farm Workers'* headquarters. We watched as they chose the families who would receive loans for housing. They aimed to select the poorest people capable of paying their bills. That's when I met *Señor Lechuga,* – Mr. Lettuce – who was in charge of the *Farm Workers'* organic-garden project. He told me his groups needed a *tractorcito* – a little tractor – to plow the seven acres of land next to the farm workers' building where they planned to grow organic vegetables to sell in cities like Austin. *Expanding Horizons* went out on a limb to support the garden project by adding $4,000 to the $2,000 Mr. Lechuga had raised from

Delivering one of the homes to its base

The first house built by Proyecto Azteca *in 1992.*
The builders (in front) sent this picture to say thank you.

other sources, thus making it possible for him to buy the *tractorcito*.

That same spring, the *Proyecto Azteca* board invited a group of us from Austin and Houston, including my cousin, Standish Meacham, to come again to celebrate the completion of the first home and to see the other changes. Right away I noticed that the black dirt around the community center was patterned with clumps of cucumber and squash plants. The community center was filled with baskets of vegetables ready to be delivered to markets. Señor Lechuga beamed as he watched us admiring the results of his work.

Nearby, the seven men who were in the original family home-building project were putting up the framework of the second and third houses. The building coordinator was helping them with details. When I asked if they could play some music during the celebration of the completion of the first home, their faces lit up, and they brought their guitars to the blessing of that first house. When we arrived we met María, whose sparkling white dress trimmed in turquoise matched her new house. She told me proudly, "I chose the colors."

Padre Miguel, a priest from Harlingen, had been invited to do the blessing. We all crowded inside to participate. A young woman with a bowl and palm branch sprinkled water on us and on the rooms as we moved through the house reading prayers for the young couple and their son in each room of the house. As the blessing ended, two of the men who had built the house began to play their accordions. Then we served ourselves bean soup, rice, guacamole, hot tortillas, and barbecued chicken, and had lunch outside in the hot sun.

It is a joy to make a difference in people's lives. I could not keep from dancing to the music played by the homebuilders. After my short dance, I felt moved to step up onto the porch of that house, to say in Spanish:

We are here to thank all of you for getting your community

off to a good start. This house will be a home not only for
you, but I pray it will encourage other families to believe
their hopes can also come true. It may even move people
from distant places to help out. Let's give thanks and pray
this home may become like a mother who will give birth to
many more like her!

Congressman Kika de la Garza and David Hall from *Texas
Rural Legal Aid* joined us for lunch. Since then, David Hall has
helped *colonia* residents with legal problems related to developers. Kika de la Garza was one of the first representatives to give
them a voice in the Texas House.

Once *colonia* residents learned their voices counted, they
began coming to the Texas State Capitol by the busload to lob-
by for themselves. In so many ways, that sparkling turquoise
trimmed white frame house did become a rallying point and a
"can do" symbol for people on the border. News spread. People who had lost hope became hopeful again.

When we got back to the airport in Austin, I noticed that
Standish was in tears. He gave me a hug and said, "This trip has
changed me for good. I want to help you in this work in every
way," and he has. The "seeing" changed him just as it did many
of those who went to Central America.

As I continued to hear more good reports about how our
initial investment had taken root, grown and spread, I thought
of Isaiah 65, one of Jorge's and my favorite biblical passages.
Like the people Isaiah tells about, the farm workers and their
families had served others for generations while they had seldom enjoyed the fruit of their labor. But, here is the reversal
Isaiah prophesied:

> They shall build houses and inhabit them;
>
>> they shall plant vineyards and eat their fruit.
>
> They shall not build and another inhabit;

Me and cousin, Standish Meacham, at a Proyecto Azteca *project site.*

Maria and I, enjoying a quiet visit on the porch of Maria's new home.

> they shall not plant and another eat;
>
> for like the days of a tree
>
> shall the days of my people be,
>
> and my chosen shall long enjoy
>
> the work of their hands.
>
> (Isaiah 65:21-22)

This kind of vision has sustained *Expanding Horizons* and *colonia* residents in South Texas.

Another way *colonia* residents played a powerful role in changing their own lives was through speaking out in public policy meetings. In 1993, members of *Proyecto Azteca* recruited a van-load of people to make the six-hour trek up to Austin to testify at a TDHCA board meeting. When Jorge and I arrived in midmorning, we noticed the *Proyecto Azteca* van was loaded with vegetables ready for delivery to Austin grocery stores. *Colonia* residents were upstairs in the TDHCA office being served coffee by Governor Ann Richards' daughter, Cecile. In the meeting, John Henneberger explained the urgency of the housing needs along the border.

Apparently our combined work was effective, because soon after these meetings, the TDHCA Board voted to make *colonia* housing a priority for state housing funds. This decision to include poor people in their lending policies was a fundamental change. Formerly TDHCA had lent money primarily to middle-class clients. This new, more expansive lending policy was a clear example of much-needed changes in the arrangements that had kept people poor. Now, TDHCA had decided to offer colonia residents zero percent interest mortgage loans for the materials to build their own homes.

Other shifts occurred when the developers' lending practices were brought into the open. Dan Morales, the Texas State Attorney General, authorized lawyers to represent *colonia* residents. They won a few cases against developers. Some developers were forced to sell their land to the *Texas State Affordable Housing Corporation*, which then lent money to *colonia* residents so they could pay on mortgages to buy land and build their own homes. Some did not believe *colonia* residents would repay their loans, but they have been proven wrong.

Press conferences were held. Reporters from all the major cities of Texas described the struggles of people along the border. Politicians realized that *colonia* residents had clout, and people from other parts of Texas became aware of the plight of their "distant neighbors." By 1994, many more people became aware that the process of contract for deed was unjust. Contract for deed was reformed by the Texas legislature in 1995. Now, when people buy land, if the sales agent talks to the buyer in Spanish, the terms of the contract must be written in Spanish. These reforms make it harder for developers to evict the owners on a whim as they did in the past.

Those of us who had prayed the "big prayer" in 1992 were surprised by God's magnanimity. That initial grant of $16,000 was like the few loaves and fishes that fed a crowd of over 5,000. It spurred the growth of the *Proyecto Azteca* board which, when we first got involved in 1991, represented only the immediate area around the town of San Juan. Four years later, *Proyecto Azteca* had grown to represent over three hundred *colonias*. Over seventy-five families had completed their own homes in community/family home-building projects sponsored by *Proyecto Azteca*. The original grant had also spawned over two million dollars in county, state and federal funds, most of which was used to loan money to poor families engaged in building their own homes. For me, this was one more confirmation of how money wisely invested can bless people's lives.

Through more articles in the press, Texans became aware of the needs of people in the *colonias*. In 1998, the *colonias* received an additional two hundred seventy-nine million dollars for water and sewer hookups from state and federal sources. Lawmakers in the Texas legislature also enacted a 5.6 million dollar loan program to help poor families along the border make repairs or build new homes if they perform some of the labor themselves.

In 1993, we went a step further. It had become clear to us that until there were community-based organizations, economic development would be done to the people, instead of with them. That is when we stopped focusing on building houses and decided to build communities of people along the Texas Mexico border. We named this venture *Iniciativa Frontera*. The point was to build local boards within *colonias* so residents could identify their own needs. Once this was done, outsiders and *colonia* residents began working together to solve problems according to priorities set by the people themselves. For the first time, *colonia* residents had a chance to determine their own lives. People who had been voiceless could finally be heard.

With this vision in mind, John Henneberger and Karen Paup, who joined him as co-director of *The Texas Low-Income Housing Information Service*, began building community organizations, modeled after *Proyecto Azteca,* all along the Texas/Mexico border. One of the first was *Colonias Unidas*, located in Starr County on the Rio Grande, halfway between Laredo and the Gulf of Mexico. The *Colonias Unidas'* board, elected by the colonia residents, decided their number-one priority was to build a community center. In June of 1994, I attended its opening. The center looked like a miniature airplane hangar, with a cement floor and a partly completed roof. It has been built each step by step. The residents asked John Henneberger and me to give $30 to build a window, and they sold one dollar raffle tickets to complete the roof.

On the way back to McAllen that night, Luis Miguel Vasquez, from the *Center for Community Change* in Washington, D.C., who had come down to Texas to help in the process of community building, told me the need for fundraising was urgent. He explained *Iniciativa Frontera* sponsors could not use government funding or they would be completely hemmed in by tedious regulations. He hoped I could raise $60,000 right away and $200,000 for the long run. For one thing, *Iniciativa Frontera* needed to hire a second field director to help in covering the 900 miles from Laredo to El Paso.

In my view, it takes years to lay the groundwork for fundraising. Standish Meacham was even less patient than Miguel Vasquez. After I told Standish what Miguel had said, he pushed me! "Gretchen, we have to get our act together. You, through *Expanding Horizons*, together with me, cannot give more than $35,000 annually. That's not enough. You have had three fundraising dinners in the past two years, but no one has contributed. Why should we limit ourselves to what appears to be possible? Let's get moving!"

I hate asking friends for money. However, I know it is essential to forget my embarrassment. It helped me to remember that we were investing directly in people's lives. In 1994 and 1995, I organized two more trips to the border for potential donors. Once people saw first-hand what was happening, they often volunteered to help. Afterwards, Standish and I set off like Robin Hoods knocking on people's doors. By June in 1995, we had raised $120,000. That would have been fine if we had been able to keep up the pace, but we were interrupted when I had a kidney removed and a partial hysterectomy in 1995. Then, in 1999, I planned another trip, which was easier, because at that point, people all over Texas, even in Washington D.C., had heard about our initiatives on the Texas border. This time, we raised over $170,000.

Through my involvement with the Texas/Mexico border, I learned once again not to be hemmed in by what appears to be feasible. I had seen that a few people could realize visions that seemed, at the outset, to be way beyond their reach. In spite of

178

★ INITIATIVE ★ DETERMINATION ★ INITIATIVE ★ DETERMINATION

Yet the colonia residents have not given up.

They do a lot with very little.

Many borrow to buy outrageously over-priced lots

    on which they build ramshakle dwellings

      out of salvaged materials.

Almost all consistently manage to pay back loans they can obtain.

MULTIPLIER EFFECT

Now, three years later, sixty-five families have built their houses, and the Proyecto Azteca Community Board has inspired the development of four more community organizations along the border.

Imagine how much more colonia residents can do if we combine our resources with their resourcefulness!

★ DETERMINATION ★ INITIATIVE   ★ DETERMINATION ★ INITIATIVE

For more information contact
Karen Paup or John Henneberger, Co-Directors
Texas Low Income Housing
Information Service

508 Powell St., Austin, Texas 78703
(512)477-8910

INICIATIVA FRONTERA

aims to improve the lives of colonia residents through building community organizations. At the heart of INICIATIVA FRONTERA is the belief that the most effective resource for solving problems in colonias is the initiative and determination of the residents to help themselves.

Taken from the *Initiativa Frontera* brochure

daunting obstacles, *colonia* residents managed to build five community organizations along the border. This means people living in those communities can now speak out through their local boards. By working together and being clear about what they need, *colonia* residents now have the means to find solutions for the lack of drinking water, sewage disposal, health care and housing. Many of us had prayed in the "big prayer" that these local boards would become pockets of hope for *colonia* residents and points of inspiration for those of us who support them, and they have.

In the mid-nineties, *Expanding Horizons* began to look for ways to get involved closer to home. That's when Jorge and I became aware of the problem facing working single mothers who needed to find child-care and development centers for their infants and young children. We learned that teachers in these centers receive such low pay that few people are willing to take these jobs.

This coincided with a period in our lives when Jorge and I had trouble sleeping. While lying in bed, holding hands, we prayed for the children. In 1995, our focus was riveted on the child-care and education center linked to our church, *El Buen Pastor.* Incredibly, soon after we began to pray, the city announced the availability of money for buildings to house early-childhood education centers. Jorge led a team effort to apply for the grant. We got a million dollars to build a new center for the children in east Austin. When I heard *El Buen Pastor* had received the grant, I laughed and said it was "our baby."

We base our planning on facts as well as feeling. Statistics seem dull, but they help us to get a view of what's happening throughout our country. I have been deeply concerned to learn that over twenty-eight percent of our children under six in Texas are living in poverty. (*The US Census Small Area Income and Poverty Estimator Program, 1994.*) These little ones have no voice, and often their parents don't either. All of the *Expanding Horizons'* board were upset not only about the plight of the children but to find out that between 1985 and 1995 the violent crime rate in the U.S. had increased sixty-six percent. (*National Kids Count Data Book, 1998.*) We were also appalled to learn that, for an American born this year (1999), the chance of living some part of life in a correction facility is 1 in 20; for black Americans, it is 1 in 4. (*New York Times, Section 4, p. 1, 3/7/1999*)

Expanding Horizons' board members decided to try to change this unhealthy national trend. Our first step was to learn more in order to focus effectively. An undertaking called the *Perry Preschool Project* (High Scope Project, Ypsilanti, Michigan) showed us there is a connection between the children who are being ignored and our huge prison population here in Texas. It also demonstrated that one way to insure that fewer children go to prison as adults, would be to improve early-childhood development centers. The *Perry Preschool* research has demonstrated that very young children who are neglected are far more likely to land in juvenile court or prison. It also showed that children who attend excellent early-child development centers that involve their parents are more likely to complete school, find worthwhile employment, own their homes, and contribute to their communities, than children who lack this opportunity.

We talked about these findings at *Expanding Horizons* board meetings. In 1996, we had our first "vision" meeting at Stony Point, my lawyer friend Bill Hilger's farm. That's when our board decided to focus our resources on improving the quality of Austin's early-child-care and education centers, giving first priority to the children in poverty.

In the fall of 1998, we invited five other foundations to join us in sponsoring a panel discussion entitled *Early Childhood at Risk*. The mayor moderated the discussion. Child-care providers and city leaders attended. That's when we began to build awareness of the need for top-notch early childhood development centers and to make plans for improving existing centers. By 1999, representatives from ten foundations, one corporation and the city had joined our collaborative.

My mother and dad have been invisible backers of *Expanding Horizons*. My father began teaching me to be a businesswoman from the age of five by paying me twenty-five cents an hour to rake leaves. A few years later, he put me in charge of the pig and chicken business. That's how I learned the importance of saving money. My mother encouraged my vision. Though she wasn't alive when *Expanding Horizons* began, her spirit was.

Epilogue

As Dad grew older, he and Jorge became closer. Humor blos-
somed in their conversations. Since Jorge is a Mexican theologian from a humble background and dad was a Texas businessman, I was surprised to see them enjoying each other so
much. This began in the early 1990's when Dad's body and
mind were waning, a period when Jorge and I often went to
Dad's home at Hickory Creek Ranch in east Texas to visit him.
Jorge realized that my Dad was a creature of his times, and that
he reflected views on race typical of Texas in the 1940's and 50's.

But also, in a strange way, Dad's natural kindness allowed these
lines to blur, as they did in the way he accepted Jorge. Jorge
noticed this and found that one of the most effective ways to
disarm him was to make fun of his views. For instance, Jorge
would taunt him with predictions that Jesse Jackson would
become president of the United States. Dad would respond,
"Yeah, yeah, then we'll all be on welfare." But he would say this
in such a devilish way that Jorge couldn't help but burst out
laughing as he said, "Tom, there is no hope for you." Then Dad
would laugh and say something like, "There is hope for me,
because you have such good connections 'upstairs,' and I'm sure
you will persuade them to forgive me."

As Dad became more dependent, Jorge always respected his
dignity and never missed a chance to be helpful to him in

practical ways. One day, Dad called me in Austin, and said, "You know, Gretchen, I really do love Jorge." Another time when Dad was with his lawyer, they called together and asked me to tell Jorge they wanted him to conduct Dad's funeral.

Several years after those longish visits to Hickory Creek, my brother Charles called late on the night of my birthday, January 10th, 1997, to tell us Dad had just died. He was almost ninety years old. Since he was ready to go, and I had silently told him good-bye hundreds of times, I told myself I had to let him go. He would not have wanted to go on living in his weakened state. Even so, I had so much wanted to be with him when he died that I had a hard time forgiving myself for not being there. My cousin and adopted sister, Sarah Shartle Meacham, said I was there, because Dad knew how much I loved him. That really helped.

In his funeral sermon, Jorge said, "Tom and I came from two very different worlds, he from the world of commerce and industry, I from the world of religion and the academy. He was a solid American; I, a Mexican immigrant." After Jorge's talk,

Me, Dad and Jorge at Hickory Creek Ranch

184

he encouraged people to tell stories. A man from the Salvation Army in Houston told us that Dad had raised over a million dollars when he was serving as chairman of the board for the Army in the seventies. He had raised that money while we were in Mexico and had never mentioned it.

Alberta Moore, who had been our housekeeper at the ranch for about fifteen years, also testified:

> Mr. Shartle was a good man, a very good man. I want to say to you children to be just like him, for he treated everybody right. Mr. Shartle was very good to our church. And this one (pointing to me) has also helped us. Their contributions bought our chairs. Now, you grandchildren comin' up, it's time for you. Follow your granddaddy and help out like he did.

My dream was and is that our family will follow Alberta's advice.

Alberta and Greta at Hickory Creek Ranch in 1997

This past June 1999, when I was on my way to my fortieth reunion at Wellesley, I thought about my life forty years before and realized how blessed I am now to feel I am on a good track. Though work sometimes overwhelms me, I now have a clearer sense of direction and no longer feel the frustration of not knowing what God is calling me to do.

I love remembering the joyful times, like dancing at dawn on the Nicaraguan border of Honduras in 1983 and dancing in the South Texas mid-day sun to the tune of the builders' guitars in 1992. Now, when I go to sleep at night, it is comforting to remember others sleeping in their good homes built by communities along the border. I am grateful for all the invisible goodness which has a life of its own, a life that multiplies and carries on for generations to come.

Kyria, Me, and Greta, December 1999